ERA

Mysterious Missing Persons
Stories From Around The World

'The lot of the one left behind is ever the harder.'
Percy Fawcett

Mark Bridgeman

Brindle Books 2023

Brindle Books Ltd

This edition published by

Brindle Books Ltd

Unit 3, Grange House

Grange Street

Wakefield

United Kingdom

WF2 8TF

ISBN 978 1 915631 10 7

Cover design by emb graphics ltd

BRINDLE

BOOKS

http://www.brindlebooks.co.uk

CONTENTS

The Legs On The Train Murder

The Real Indiana Jones

Author's Note:

Erased is a uniquely interactive and enhanced book, perhaps the world's first unique bridge between the paperback and the ebook – the truly enhanced paperback, or e-back. New information will be added whenever it is available, meaning for years to come, the stories will remain fresh and updated. This extra e-information is only available to owners of the paperback version of Erased, making this book uniquely interactive and never out of date.

The Erased e-back provides much more information than you might normally expect to find within the pages of a paperback. In tandem with each story, you will find QR codes and links, which will allow the reader to instantly access exclusive bonus photographs and extra content relating to that story.

Chapters four and five of *Erased* take place in the underbelly of 1940s Los Angeles, beneath Tinseltown's respectable surface. I have included lots of references to the hardboiled film noirs of the period. I wonder how many you can spot?

These is also an exclusive competition with a bag of goodies available to the winner. This can only be accessed via the QR code at the end of the book. Good luck!

As a special extra there is an additional *Erased* story, only available via a secret website. You will also find a QR code tucked away at the back of this book.

Welcome to the world of the enhanced paperback.

In addition, at the conclusion of the book there is a page entitled 'The Search Continues' which will enable you to find updates to missing persons cases and to access official missing persons databases around the globe. Many of these organisations rely on charitable donations and the good will of the public. Please remember, some of the content may be upsetting and may require age verification. The content may not necessarily agree with the opinion of the author, but does provide other perspectives on the various stories contained in the book.

If you would like to report someone missing, or if you feel you can provide any information on an existing case, you will also be able to do so here. Someone, somewhere in the world may hold the key that unlocks an unsolved missing persons mystery.

If you do not already have a QR code scanner on your smartphone, you can easily download a free version from your Appstore. Once you have done so, simply open the app, hold the scanner over the QR code, and you will be taken directly to the appropriate information.

All photographs used are in the public domain, or the original copyright is unknow. Please be aware, some of the content contains archaic expressions no longer used.

Introduction

'Light thinks it travels faster than anything, but it is wrong. No matter how fast light travels, it finds the darkness has always got there first, and is waiting for it.'
Terry Pratchett

Each year, more than 500,000 people are reported missing in the United States. In the United Kingdom the figure is approximately 170,000. One every 90 seconds. Although many are found, or return home safely, roughly one in five cases remain active. At any one time, the FBI's National Crime Information Center (NCIC) holds well over 90,000 active or ongoing cases, officially classified as 'Missing Person and Unidentified Person Files.'

The number is quite simply both staggering and heart-breaking. Yet our fascination with these tragic tales perhaps reveals as much about our own sense of fragility and fear as it does about the stories we read. How could this happen? How can someone simply disappear? We cannot help but wonder.

Our sense of wonderment is perhaps only surpassed by our sense of dark curiosity. What really happened to the individual in question? This book presents seven absorbing and intriguing cases from across the world. Some provide closure, some do not.

That is the nature of an abrupt and unexpected disappearance. We may never know all the answers. Perhaps that is also part of their everlasting appeal and fascination.

Mark Bridgeman

www.markbridgemanauthor.co.uk

"Exempt from death is he who takes his life;
My time has come."
John Davidson, 1908

Part One:

Douglas Sherrin Frith Panton was born into an artistic and financially successful family at Wareham in Dorset during the summer of 1875. He enjoyed a healthy and prosperous rural childhood. When still a young boy, his family moved to a large property, The Manor House, at Wayside, on the Hempstead Road leading to Watford. The new home allowed his father, James, to concentrate on his role as Managing Director of Benskin's Brewery in Watford, and his mother, Jane E. Panton, to pursue her literary aspirations. Clearly affluent, the Panton's took on a gardener, butler, cook, kitchen maid, parlour maid, Lady's maid and house maid. Douglas benefited from a good education too, firstly at Harrow School, and then at Cambridge, as did his brother.

His mother published several works including the successful *Leaves from a Life* and *Suburban Residences*. His grandfather William Powell Frith was a painter of some repute and a fellow of the Royal Academy, whilst his uncle, Walter Frith, penned many well-received novels and plays including *The Tutor's Love Story, In Search of Quiet, The Man of Forty, and The Iron Duke*. It seems, Douglas Panton continued his family's artistic leanings. While studying at

Cambridge, he indulged in amateur dramatics and even joined the prestigious Footlights Review. However, ultimately, it appears he did not wish to follow in his family's footsteps; choosing instead to study law.

After finding employment as an articles clerk in 1893, he continued to work studiously. Panton soon passed the bar and soon moved permanently to London. He became a partner in the firm of Camp, Ellis and Panton Solicitors, in Bedford Row in the City. Still only thirty years of age, employed in a respected practice in a handsome row of Georgian houses in the heart of London, Panton's life seemed complete. London was the heart of the British Empire. The new King, Edward, had embraced the Capital as a city of culture and learning, the Olympics came to London, and thousands flocked to see the Franco-British Exhibition and the Summer of Sport. Panton even found time to please his mother by regularly attending music hall shows, by joining a small amateur theatrical society, and by taking a fashionable townhouse in Loudoun Road, St John's Wood. Yet, somewhere behind the brick-walled, leafy gardened respectability of St John's Wood, a dark spectre seemed to lurk in the recesses of his mind.

Gossip began to spread among his work colleagues and in his social circle. A rumour circulated that Panton enjoyed reading, what was disapprovingly referred to at the time as, 'sensational literature' and 'flagellation poetry' (poetry concerned with flogging, beating, or self-punishment, usually as a form of religious punishment or sexual gratification).

Bedford Row

Thoroughly disapproved of by polite Edwardian society, Panton was also rumoured to have a collection of banned novels and postcards featuring dead bodies and bizarre acts of suicide. A colleague claimed to have seen some photographs in his possession, one of a woman lying dead at the foot of a cliff, entitled *Leaping to Her Death*, another of a woman taking her own life by jumping from a bridge.

Panton gradually became unreliable at work too, taking long periods of time off sick, which he usually explained away as '*suffering from another bout of influenza*', although many were as the result of long hours spent at his London club, or mixing with 'theatrical types'. His parents also became aware of these long absences and the adverse effect they had on his standing as a solicitor. He missed important meetings with clients, costing his partnership both a loss of reputation and of revenue.

Eventually, matters reached a head in March of 1908. He was summoned by the other partners at the firm and, following a heated meeting, it was decided to dismiss him. He was now unemployed, with a large house in St John's Wood to maintain, together with an expensive bachelor's lifestyle. Panton desperately attempted to keep his embarrassed financial status a secret from his family, however, gradually he began to show signs of the burden now pushing down on his fragile shoulders. His behaviour became erratic and his mood swings noticeable to all around him. Eventually, in early March 1909, his brother, Phillip, decided to pay Douglas a visit in London. He would later tell the police, *'When I last saw Douglas at the beginning of March, he was terribly distressed, as if something dreadful had happened. He did not seem himself, evidently, I now know that his mind had become deranged.'*

Finally, the strain appears to have become too great for the young unemployed solicitor. At some point, shortly after meeting his brother in early March, he simply vanished. With no wife to report him missing, nor a current employer, his absence was not noticed for several days. During that period, he may have been in London, both alive and well. Nevertheless, there were no confirmed sightings of him, he did not attend his club, nor did he contact his family. After ten days, worried about their son's mental state, his mother and father wired a telegram from Watford:

'Dearest Douglas. Are you well? No reply to our enquiries. Phillip will call tomorrow. – J.A.P.'

To their great surprise, despite their previous messages having gone unanswered, they received a response on

Monday 19th April, wired from a telegraph office in Holburn:

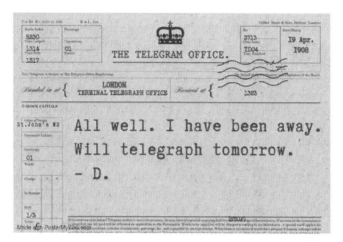

However, the following day brought no new communication from their son. Another day passed, then another, and another. Now distraught with worry, and believing that Douglas was not able to deal with his pressing financial affairs, his family paid a visit to Panton's home in Loudoun Road, St John's Wood. When they arrived, it was immediately clear that the house was unoccupied. Mail had piled up and the fires had not been lit for many days. They immediately decided to call into the St John's Wood police station and report their son missing. After explaining the chain of events, a description of the missing man was communicated to the London press,

'Douglas S. F. Panton:- Age 33; height 5 feet 5 inches; fair complexion, hair fair, build thin. At the time of his disappearance he was believed to be wearing either a tweed or blue serge suit. His family believe him to be in great distress and unable to manage his affairs.'

The Metropolitan Police spent seven days making exhaustive enquiries, contacting solicitors' offices, gentleman's clubs, public houses, the London Solicitors' Golf Club, and post offices throughout London. The wealth and relatively high profile of Panton's family ensured that every effort was made to secure his safe return. It was revealed that Panton had been a keen amateur golfer, with a handicap of five, however, he had let his membership of the Solicitors' Golf Club lapse. Similarly, it was also discovered that he had previously frequented the Rhymers' Club (a literary society founded by the poet W.B Yeats), possibly due to his interest in literature, or perhaps through his family's connections with the society. It is probable that he met the Scottish poet and playwright, John Davidson, who had relocated to London, either at the Rhymers' Club, at a London Theatre, or through his literary mother and uncle. John Davidson, it seems, would have a profound influence on the unfolding events.

Unfortunately, other than the telegraph clerk at Holburn Post Office who had recognised Douglas Panton's description, there were no other confirmed sightings of the missing man. The London newspapers gave his disappearance the zest of sensationalism, in an effort to sell extra copies, some lurid speculation followed, including links to gambling debts, to bizarre suicide pacts, and to a missing woman (described as being '*of dubious moral character*').

Feeling that Panton may have taken his own life, the London River Police were asked to search the Thames (which was notorious as the watery graveyard in which many a distressed soul would choose to end their life). However, this also proved fruitless, as did as a check of all the London hospitals. Meanwhile, another week passed without any further news of the missing man.

In this golden age of crime (fuelled by the latest Sherlock Holmes stories and the 'penny dreadful' crime novels sold at railway station bookstalls) the public's insatiable appetite for sensational mysteries shifted to two other stories which dominated the headlines. Firstly, the disappearance of the Scottish poet John Davidson seemed to make a more newsworthy story than that of an obscure London solicitor. Davidson, who similarly to Douglas Panton, was burdened with financial difficulties as well as illness, had left London and moved to Penzance in Cornwall towards the end of 1908. He was last seen there on 23rd March 1909, three days after the last known sighting of Douglas Panton in London. Although Davidson enjoyed some success as a writer, poet, and playwright, he had suffered from severe cashflow problems. These issues continued, despite being granted a civil list pension of £100 per annum, at the recommendation of George Bernard Shaw. The onset of cancer followed, leading Davidson into a spiral of hopelessness and clinical depression, resulting in his disappearance on 23rd March.

A fellow member of the Rhymers' Club issued an appeal and description to the London newspapers, in the hope that Davidson might be found alive:

'John Davidson is a little below middle height, but strongly built with square shoulders and remarkably fine face and head; the features were almost classically

regular, the eyes dark brown and large, the forehead high, the hair and moustache black. His manners are both frank and natural.'

Davidson's family and friends decided to offer a substantial reward of £20 (approximately £3,000 today), for information leading to the discovery of the missing writer. Posters were placed around Penzance and at railway stations between Cornwall and the capital.

There seemed to be little doubt among Davidson's family that he had taken his own life. His wife, Margaret, found a letter next to a manuscript on his desk, which contained the statement, *'This will be my last work.'* Indeed, this theory seemed to be confirmed in an anthology entitled *The Testament of John Davidson* (published a year earlier in 1908), in which the poet appears to have anticipated his own fate:

> *'None should outlive his power. . . . Who kills*
> *Himself subdues the conqueror of kings;*
> *Exempt from death is he who takes his life;*
> *My time has come."*

Although, at the time of either man's disappearance, no potential connection between them was known. Nevertheless, a number of coincidences seemed to tie their fortunes together. However, before any link could be made by the authorities in the hunt for either of the men, an unexpected twist changed the course of both investigations.

By 23rd April 1909, there had not been a single confirmed sighting of either man, for almost a month.

Cornish police had searched the coastline around Penzance, on the assumption that John Davidson had taken his own life (Davidson's wife, Margaret, had informed the police that her husband's wish had always been for a burial at sea). Meanwhile in London, every known haunt of Douglas Panton had been visited by the Metropolitan Police. Publicly, the authorities wondered if he was sheltering at the home of a female friend, afraid of the shame caused by his mounting debts. Privately, however, the rumours of Panton's fascination with explicit and sensational literature caused the authorities much concern. Following the cases involving Oscar Wilde, the Suffragettes, the murder of Caroline Luard in Kent, and many others, there was little appetite amongst cabinet ministers and senior police officers for the fabric of Edwardian society to be frayed by yet more controversy and sleaze.

Finally, on the afternoon of Friday 23rd April 1909, a welcome lead presented itself in the search for Douglas Panton. Joseph Thomas, a porter at Penzance Railway Station in Cornwall, noticed a man alighting from the Paddington express. At the turn of the twentieth-century, missing persons posters and flyers were a common sight at post offices, and at the bookstalls and noticeboards of railway stations. They were easily distributed via the rail network and likely to be seen by great many people. Among the large number of passengers leaving the carriages that lunchtime, the porter's attention was attracted to one particular gentleman, due to the large, battered, and obviously heavy portmanteau which the man was manoeuvring along the platform with some difficulty, while simultaneously attempting to move hurriedly through the station concourse. The porter offered to assist; however, the man refused and had seemed clearly annoyed by the unwelcome intrusion. Something reminded the porter of a description he had seen on one of missing persons posters displayed at the station. He contacted the local police constable, P.C. Whells, and described the man as,

'A short, slim man of about 35. He was dressed in a well-worn grey suit and struggling with a large case that had evidently done much service.'

While the description appeared to closely match the earlier one given of Douglas Panton, the porter initially thought the man might have been John Davidson, the missing poet. However, the porter's account of the man does seem to differ significantly from the following description of Davidson which was displayed prominently the station's noticeboard at the time,

'Age 51 years; height about 5 feet 5 inches; stout build; dark complexion; full round pale face; brown piercing eyes, dark hair, imperial moustache tingled with grey; bald on top of head; has a varicose vein in left leg, and a mark where a wart has been removed from the finger on left hand. Dressed when he left home in a blue serge suit, dark overcoat, bowler hat, and black, buttoned boots. Davidson always carries one eyeglass, is well known as a literary man, walks very quickly, and has the appearance of a Frenchman.'

Conceivably the porter had only paid attention to the detail *'walks very quickly'*, or perhaps his view had been slightly obscured by the steam and smoke from the engine, which had not yet dispersed from the platform. Yet interestingly, despite speaking to the man, the porter made no reference to his accent.

£20 REWARD

To any person or persons giving definite information which will lead to the discovery of the whereabouts and the ultimate finding of

JOHN DAVIDSON,

missing from his home in Penzance since 7 p.m. on the 23rd March, 1909.

Age 51 years; height about 5 feet 5 ins.; stout build; dark complexion; full round pale face; brown piercing eyes; dark hair, moustache, and imperial tinged with grey; bald on top of head; has a varicose vein in left leg, and a mark where a wart has been recently removed from first finger on left hand.

Dressed when he left home in a blue serge suit, dark overcoat, bowler hat, and black buttoned boots.

DAVIDSON always carries one eyeglass, is well known as a literary man, walks very quickly, and has the appearance of a Frenchman.

It is feared that he may be suffering from loss of memory, or some ill may have befallen him.

Any information respecting the above communicate immediately to

PENZANCE,
1st April, 1909.

H. KENYON,
Head Constable.

BEARE & SON, STEAM PRINTERS, PENZANCE.

He did, however, recall the initial 'D' embossed on the man's luggage. Unfortunately, he could not remember any of the other lettering on the man's portmanteau, nor was he sure if the man caught a two-wheeler cab from Station Road or if he had exited the area on foot. Nevertheless, the detail regarding the cumbersome portmanteau case was an intriguing one and would soon become an important clue in a strange and gruesome discovery.

Part Two:

On Friday 30th April events took an unexpected and macabre turn. It had been a particularly cold beginning to the month, with freezing temperatures overnight. At dusk, a quarryman named William Johns, having finished his shift at the quarry, was walking through the meadow that meets the rocks at Penlee Point, a coastal headland at the entrance to Plymouth Sound, between Penzance and the fishing village of Mousehole. As darkness was beginning to gather, Johns was grateful to have finished work for the day. As he made his way to the coastal footpath he happened to glance down at the rocky shoreline where something caught his eye. In the shadows of the sunset, Johns noticed an object by the rocks on the shore. As he scrambled down the rocks, moving closer, he realised that the object was a body. Strangely, he had not noticed anything earlier in the day. Perhaps, he thought to himself, the body had been washed in on the high tide, then left stranded on the rocks as the waters receded. As he approached in the shadowy twilight, he noticed that the body was that of a woman, lying face down among the rocks. The lifeless corpse was dressed in a fitted jacket, long skirt and dancing shoes, although Johns could not make out the victim's face which was obscured by her long, straggly wet hair and by a copious amount of blood which covered the left side of the head. However, the most shocking aspect of the gruesome scene, which made William Johns recoil in horror, was the victim's hands – they had been manacled together with handcuffs. He then glanced down at the poor woman's ghostly pale legs, and noticed to his horror that both her feet had also been linked and bound together in an identical fashion. He recoiled both in shock and dismay at the thought of such a frightening spectacle and, without approaching any closer, he decided to run to Mousehole, the nearest village and inform P.C. Whells, the local police constable. Penlee Point was a far lonelier location than it appears today, and Johns understandably had no wish to remain there alone.

By the time P.C. Whells received Johns' report it was now night-time. Whells decided that any investigation of the crime scene would be more successful in the low tide and the revealing daylight of the early morning. High tide at Penlee Point would be reaching by lunchtime, giving the police a few hours in which to search for clues. In the meantime, he communicated with Chyandour Police Station in Penzance for any recently filed notifications of missing women in the area; however, none had been reported. William Johns, although he had not taken a close look at the body, confirmed that the woman appeared to have died only recently. Perhaps, he conjectured, the woman's body had washed ashore from further along the coast, or conceivably the victim had been forcibly abducted elsewhere, and then brought to Penlee Point against her will. It seemed a dark mystery, and P.C. Whells decided to summon as much help as possible in order to conduct a thorough search of Penlee Point at daylight the following morning.

As the sun rose on Saturday morning a search team led by P.C. Whells, the coastguard, and William Johns arrived at Penlee Point. The woman's body was unmoved from its position of the night before; but daylight revealed a scattering of other debris on the shoreline and among the rocks. With trepidation, P.C. Whells turned over the manacled body of the woman in the hope that a proper identification could be obtained. To his shock and horror, the limp corpse was actually not a woman at all, but that of a young man.

Dressed as it was in a woman's tight fitting brown jacket and skirt, long theatrical wig and dancing shoes, quite naturally the body was easily mistaken as female, even from a short distance away. Coupled with the pale skin and recently clean-shaven face and legs it was clear that a significant effort had been made to hide the victim's sexuality. In fact, the disguise was so perfect, definite identification of the body as male was not confirmed until the body was taken to Mousehole.

Obviously, the manacled hands and legs ruled out any sort of accidental death or drowning. The unknown victim had not only died in the most sinister of circumstances; but an effort had been made to conceal their gender, for reasons which would need to be established.

Due to the reported disappearance of John Davidson from nearby Penzance, as soon as the body was confirmed as male, the natural assumption was made that the unidentified corpse belonged to the missing poet. However, a search of the surrounding rocky shoreline soon yielded a bounty of other clues. First to be discovered was a man's striped shirt bearing the label 'Messrs. T. Hugo and Sons, Outfitters, Penzance' and a waistcoat. Next to be uncovered was a pair of Connemara stone cufflinks, of which the link in one had been broken at some point, and been replaced with a bone toothpick. This led P.C. Whells, no doubt influenced by the latest collection of Sherlock Holmes stories, to deduce that the owner of the DIY-repaired cufflinks had once enjoyed a degree of wealth but, while maintaining some self-respect, had now fallen on hard times. The man's shirt from Penzance and the cufflinks initially appeared to strengthen the assumption that the body may have been that of John Davidson; however, the discovery of a torn scrap of paper bearing the word 'Panton' and part of an address '__doun Road, St ____W', convinced the police that the corpse must be that of the missing London solicitor Douglas Panton. A closer examination of the body also seemed to fit this theory, as the height and build of the victim appeared much closer to the description of Panton than to that of Davidson. To confirm their hypothesis a telegram was sent by Inspector Warring of the Cornwall County Constabulary to Scotland Yard, requesting help in identified the body:

'Body found at Penzance apparently that of Panton, reported missing London. Request assistance in identification by family. C.C.C. 2 May.'

Scotland Yard in turn contacted the Panton family in London, who cabled the following communication to Penzance:

'Brother leaves Paddington 9.50 evening, second class, for Penzance to identify body. Arrives 7.30 tomorrow morning.'

Douglas Panton's brother, Phillip, was met at Penzance station by Inspector Warring. A number of reporters had also gathered there hoping to secure a scope for their respective newspapers. Before any questions could be asked, the pair were whisked away in a waiting motor car and driven to a small wooden hut in Mousehole, overlooking the harbour, where the body of the victim had been moved.

After identifying the body Phillip Panton gave a statement to the small crowd that had congregated in the fishing harbour,

'My first fears are now confirmed. I have no doubt at all that the dead man is my brother, Mr Douglas Sherrin Frith Panton.'

In the meantime, the Cornish police had not been idle. Officers visited various hotels and guesthouses in the Penzance area in an attempt to locate where the dead man might have been staying. John Davidson's house in Coulsons Terrance, Penzance, was also checked, however no proof could be found that Panton had visited there. Davidson had already been missing for over a month and the police had naturally wondered if the two deaths were linked. Fortunately, it was not long before another breakthrough came in this perplexing mystery. James Roxburgh, the head 'boots' at the

Queen's Hotel on the Western Promenade Road in Penzance, recognised the description of Douglas Panton as a guest who had checked in at the hotel on the previous Friday (23rd April). The man had signed the hotel's register under the name 'D. Platton.' James Roxburgh was able to confirm that the man had been not seen at the hotel since Monday 26th April, having informed the concierge that he would not be back that night and that his room was to be left undisturbed. However, after a few days had passed, and the Queen's Hotel had still not received any communication from 'Mr Platton', they had naturally become concerned. The police immediately entered the guest's room and made a full search of Mr Platton's belongings, including a large portmanteau embossed with the letters D.S.F.P.

On opening the portmanteau (on which a crude attempt had been made to scratch off the lettering) the police officers were greeted with a treasure trove of clues to help explain the strange disappearance of the missing solicitor. A complete list was made of the contents, a copy of which still exists, and which reads as follows:

'A cardboard box with label of Clarkson (famous London wig makers), grease paints, perfumes, box with beaded pins, box of complexion soap, small silver match box, small tape measure, three reels of cotton, comb, scissors, pocketknife, two military hair brushes, sponge bag, paper covered novel, several copies of Society, Daily Mail, Western Morning News, Illustrated Police Budget and Photo Bits. A clothes brush, two handkerchiefs (one with the initials F.H. in corner), several collars in collar box, well-stocked

needle case, pair of socks, pair of light blue pants, woollen undervest, a striped shirt (name of makers cut away), pyjamas, small lounge coat (grey material) – nothing in the pockets. The word "Wayland" and "Watford" were written on the inside of the case, but faded and difficult to read.'

Cornish police were never able to trace or identify the owner of the handkerchief bearing the monogram 'F.H.'

This strange assortment of items appeared to indicate someone who had clearly intended to disguise themselves as a woman. However, any suggestion that the missing man may have, in anyway, indulged in cross-dressing was not mentioned in any contemporary report or newspaper article. This was considered far too distasteful for public consumption. Curiously, therefore, the possibility that Douglas Panton, before taking his own life, intended to dress in female clothing purely as a form of elaborate disguise, was considered to be the only possible reason for his extravagant wardrobe. The fact that he may have been murdered (in what might now called a 'hate crime'), or perhaps was being blackmailed, or a transvestite, were never publicly considered or debated.

James Roxburgh, having seen Douglas Panton at the Queens Hotel, was able to provide a crucial second positive identification of the body at Mousehole. Mr Frederick Hugo, from Hugo and Sons Outfitters, was also able to confirm that Mr Panton had visited his shop in Penzance during the previous week and purchased some new collars and a shirt. Armed with this information the local magistrate was able to call an official inquest into the death of the London solicitor. With John Davidson still missing at this stage, the investigation into his disappearance would remain open.

The inquest was held in the United Methodist Church schoolroom in Mousehole on Thursday 6th May under the jurisdiction of the County Coroner, Mr Edward Boase. He opened the proceeding by addressing the inquest jury,

'Mr Craddock (who had been elected foreman of the inquest jury)*, we are gathered here to inquire into the circumstances attending the death of Mr Douglas Sherrin Frith Panton. The fact that the body, although that of a male, was dressed in female clothing, made the case somewhat different from those which we ordinarily investigate, but I have no doubt that you will be able to gather from the evidence that this disguise was apparently used for the purpose of concealing his identity.'*

William Johns, the man who had first seen the body, identified himself as a *'stone breaker, of Cherry Garden Street, Mousehole'*, and testified as follows,

'Between the rocks on the Mousehole side of Penlee Point, I found a body lying dry. I made no examination of the body myself, sir, but reported the matter to the constable. The head was towards the shore, and at first I thought it was a woman.'

P.C. Whells gave evidence next, *'About 7.30pm on Friday I was told that a body was lying on the western shore. I went to the spot in the morning and found the body, which was clothed as a woman, lying between two rocks. There was no water round the body, the tide being low. An examination of the body showed it to that of a man. I telephoned to Inspector Warring and removed the body to the building opposite the Ship Hotel. There were handcuffs on the wrists, of a self-locking pattern, and the legs were manacled.*

On Saturday at 11am Dr Miller made a post-mortem examination, and I was present that morning when the body was identified as Mr Panton. We searched the rocks on Saturday morning, and about 100 yards from where the body was discovered I found a walking stick, a nickel bangle, a pair of trousers, and one boot. The trousers were at the high-water mark and the boot about two feet below that. The bangle was much below the high-water mark. About 20 feet away from these articles there were several scraps of paper. Some bore such words as "hat" and "veil", and one had the word "Panton" on it. A lot of cigarettes ends were scattered about. I also found a matchbox.

Mr Roxburgh, the head boots of the Queen's Hotel identified the trousers and walking stick and said to me that he was satisfied that they belonged to the visitor missing from the Queen's Hotel.'

Mr Boase, the Coroner, then asked P.C. Whells a salient question, based on the constable's experience of the waters around Plymouth Sound, *'Constable Whells can you form any opinion as to how the body, found in that position, got into the water?'*

'My opinion, sir, is that he came in from the end of the Point, 100 yards away, dressed himself in the female clothes and then went across the rocks to the lower side. I think he strewed the paper about and then went down the gully, across the rocks and climbed onto Penlee Point. In coming back, he slipped and fell on the wet rocks.'

'What did you find on the beach, constable?'

'Near the spot where the body was, we found a waistcoat, a shirt, and a handkerchief. However, there were no marks on the clothing which could have led us to an immediate identification, sir.'

'And the clothing was wet, I understand, constable?'

'Yes, they had evidently been in the water, sir.'

'For how long, do you think?' asked the coroner.

'Not long, by the face of the deceased.' P.C. Whells replied.

Next to give evidence to the inquest was James Roxburgh, the head 'boots' at the Queen's Hotel,

'The man, who registered under the name of "D. Platton", arrived at the hotel on Friday week, by the Riveria Express from London. He left at 8.30 on Monday evening and did not return. This occasioned no surprise at the time, sir, because visitors often stayed out all night fishing. But, as he had returned two or three days later we lodged this information at the police station. Although, we did not know it was the same man who was missing from London.'

'You had no way of knowing that this man was, in fact, Douglas Panton, Mr Roxburgh?'

'No, sir. He signed the register as "D. Platton", and I only saw later that on his bag, nearly obliterated, were the words "D.S.F.P." and "Watford". These could only be made out with a magnifying glass and every label on his clothing had been cut away. Also, sir, we expected him back at the hotel because he had not settled his bill.'

'Very well, thank you Mr Roxburgh.'

Next, Dr Miller, the police surgeon for the district, testified, revealing some remarkable evidence from his post-mortem examination of the body,

'The most important fact was that the victim's neck was broken. Otherwise, there was also a dislocation of the first and second top cervical bones of the spine. They were completely dislocated and that would cause instant death. There were also bruises on the forehead, face, under the eyebrows, and on the nose. A deep jagged tear on the upper eyelid was also noted.

There were several bruises on the parts of the body covered with clothes. The victim's lungs were expanded, and there was no sign of death from drowning, either from the lungs or from any other organ in the body.'

Mr Boase then asked Dr Miller, 'Were the marks on the body caused before death or after?'

'Some just before, some after.'

'Were they caused by a fall, then, doctor?'

'Yes. The bruises extended from about two inches behind the top of the forehead, over the forehead and the upper part of the face. In my opinion, they were inflicted by a heavy fall, either by the falling of an object onto the body, or the body onto an object.'

'Doctor, can you express an opinion as to how long the body had been in the water?'

'That is a big matter. Because, in the first place, there was no sign of drowning, and, in my opinion, there was no sign of death having taken place more than 48 hours before I saw the body. Rigor mortis had hardly commenced. The victim's eyeball was firm and not flabby. which generally sets in about 24 hours later. There was no sign of prolonged immersion in water visible from the palms or soles of the feet. The heart was contracted, and the stomach was empty. The opening from the stomach to the bowels was contracted, which showed that the deceased had been a good many hours without food.'

'And give you give a definite cause of death, doctor?'

'Yes, I am satisfied that the cause of death is through dislocation of the neck. I could see no signs of the deceased having bled to death. There were no marks which would lead one to infer there had been a criminal assault. The marks I found on the body satisfied me that death was the result of a fall.'

'Doctor Miller, if the bruises on the body were not caused by a criminal assault, were they likely inflicted by the body washing against the rocks?'

'The bruises were not inflicted after death but, in my opinion, as a result of a fall.'

'Thank you, doctor.'

Phillip Panton, the victim's brother, informed the inquest that he had formally identified the body as that of his brother,

'I last saw him a few weeks ago. His age was 35. He was last seen by anyone who knew him on April 19th, I believe. Since then, nobody has known where he was. My brother's mental condition had been unstable for some time; so much so, that it had been necessary for the rest of the family to control, to a certain extent, his business transactions. The family had also decided that he should live at home, and not alone. He had not been able to practice as a solicitor and had held no responsible position for some months.

He had financial troubles and I do not think my brother had any money on him beyond a small amount. Although he had been depressed at times, he had not hinted at suicide.'

'Mr Panton, have you ever known him to dress in female attire?'

'No, sir.'

With the testimonies concluded, the coroner summed up the evidence for the jury,

'Gentleman of the jury, in a case of this description, there are always three possibilities of death: 1), violence by some other persons, 2), accidental, and, 3) by his own act. There is nothing in the evidence to suggest that death was caused by the act of another person. In fact. the evidence is quite contrary to that. With regard to the second possibility, you should ignore certain facts which point to the extreme probability that death was an accident, when you take in account the preparations made by the deceased in handcuffing himself and putting links on his legs, and the evidence from the hotel and from the victim's brother.

There was evident intention not only to conceal his identity from the time he left London, but also from the time he left the Queen's Hotel. And this was apparently done with the idea of putting an end to his life. It is also probable that the deceased imagined by getting into the water his body would be carried to a sufficient distance which would prohibit the association of the articles left on the beach with him. If he had intended merely to disappear it is difficult to see why he would have chosen that particular spot.

And why should he have tied himself up in that manner? It appears that he did so for the purpose of expediting his own death, by saving a certain amount

of struggling, or to prevent him changing his mind with that natural impulse of a man trying to prevent himself from drowning. I understand, from the victim's brother, that the deceased man was an excellent swimmer.

He undoubtedly took his own life while of unsound mind. No rational man would think that his true sex would remain undisclosed with the discovery of his body.'

After a short deliberation the jury returned a verdict of *'Suicide while of unsound mind.'*

Douglas Panton's body was not returned to his family in London for burial. His remains were interred at Paul Cemetery in Cornwall on the Tuesday following the inquest. Unusually, the newspapers published a complete list of the twenty people who attended the funeral, showing us that (other than his brother Phillip, who had remained in Penzance after the inquest), not a single member of his family journeyed from London to attend the service. The Rev. R.W. Aitken presided and expressed his astonishment that, *'Few people ever thought of thanking God for the gift of reason.'*

The breastplate on the deceased man's coffin bore the simple inscription,

'Douglas S.F. Patton, died April 26th, 1909, aged 35 years.'

On the day following the funeral in Cornwall, a London newspaper reporter revealed to his readers that he had *'discovered the shopping establishment in*

London' where Panton had purchased the female clothing in which his lifeless body had been found,

'It is the well-known West End supplier to the theatrical profession, known as Mademoiselle Bessie Victors in Charing Cross Road, nearly opposite the Hippodrome. Mme. Victor at first could not remember having sold a costume such as the one which has been described, but throwing her memory back, she remembered that on the morning of April 19th (the day on which Mr Panton disappeared) a gentleman, whose description tallies exactly with that of the drowned man, went into her shop and asked her for a costume for a lady "about your own build, not too long, with a 22- inch waist." She showed him a brown one trimmed with two rows of black braid, and with a black satin waistcoat, and also several others of varying price. He. however. liked the first one first shown him. and on Mme. Victor asking him if she should try the jacket on for him to see. he replied, "if you would". Mme. Victor, who is about medium height, and of good figure, put the jacket on for her customer to see. He then remarked that he thought it would suit his lady nicely. He also bought a white delaine blouse with a frill down the front. Asked if they should be sent anywhere for him, the man replied that would take them with him. and the bill was made out as follows – "1 brown cloak costume -, £2 10 shillings, 1 blouse, 6 shilling and sixpence, Total £2 16s 6d." This he paid, then asking that the goods might be packed in as small a parcel as possible. They were then put Into a cardboard box bearing the name and address of the firm on the cover, measuring 14 inches wide, 7 inches long, and 3 inches deep.'

And so, the bizarre mystery surrounding the disappearance of Douglas Panton reached its conclusion. Although the strange circumstances surrounding his death do not appear to have been investigated with any great depth. Rather, it seems a hasty conclusion to the proceedings was required for the sake of respectability. Several questions regarding the unusual position of the body and the exact chain of events were not questioned. The series of coincidences relating to the simultaneous disappearance of John Davidson were not tallied at the time and, in fact, the two deaths were never officially linked. The disappearance of a small revolver from among Davidson's personal possessions was also not discovered until much later.

The family of John Davidson would have to wait a further four months until finally learning the fate of the Scottish poet. On Saturday 18th September 1909 the decomposed body of a man was discovered at 'Carn Dhu' (the Black Rock) by a fishing vessel returning its catch to Mousehole harbour. The remains had attracted a flock of gulls which in turn caught the eye of the two fishermen, James Lawson and Orlando Humphreys. They towed the remains of the poet into the harbour at Mousehole and informed the authorities.

Although identification of the actual remains would have been made difficult due to the length of time the body had spent in the water, the pockets of the victim's clothing revealed a pipe, a packet of tobacco, a silver matchbox, an ivory letter opener, and some scraps of paper. Importantly, his revolver was not among the contents of his pockets. Mr Davidson's son, Menzies, was able to identify the objects as belonging to his father.

The inquest into John Davidson's death revealed that the poet had left his home on the evening of 22nd March, telling his family that he intended to post a manuscript of his latest poetry collection to his publisher, Mr Grant Richards. After stopping at The Star Inn for a whisky, he was not seen again; and the manuscript never reached his publisher. Although his wife, Margaret, had already found the letter referred to earlier, containing the words 'This will be my last book', another search among Davidson's papers was made. Finally, wrapped in a parcel and carefully hidden under a mountain of papers the missing manuscript was uncovered. The collection, which was to be known as *Fleet Street: And Other Poems*, contained a short preface in which the following passage caught his wife's eye,

'The time has come to make an end. There are several motives. I find my pension is not enough; I have therefore still to turn aside and attempt things for which people will pay. My health also counts. Asthma and other annoyances I have tolerated for years; but I cannot put up with cancer.'

For the purposes of determining a cause of death, Dr Miller was once again asked to perform a post-mortem on the badly decomposed remains,

'I was only able to form an assumption as to the cause of death. There was a fracture of the forehead bone about two-thirds of an inch above the eyebrows, and a small hole, about half an inch in diameter, in the right

temple. On the opposite side of the forehead there was a rather irregular hole, perhaps an inch in diameter. This small hole was such as would be made by a bullet fired from a pistol if the weapon was held to the forehead.'

The coroner thanked Dr Miller and in his summation instructed the jury that, *'it must be assumed that death was caused by a bullet, but that it could not be said who fired the shot.'*

After a short deliberation, a verdict of 'Found dead' was returned, and John Davidson was buried at sea in the waters of Mount's Bay, off Penzance, in line with his wishes.

And the intriguing mystery of the solicitor, the poet, and the lady who wasn't, drew to a close. Yet, it left many unanswered questions; particularly as the two men had almost certainly become acquainted through their membership of the Rhymers' Club and their mutual interest in 'sensational' literature and 'flagellation poetry'. Perhaps the two men had agreed a bizarre suicide pact, in which they would simultaneously take their own lives? It is even possible that Panton shot Davidson, then left their bodies to be washed out to sea together, only for his own body to return to shore, while Davidson's drifted out into the Sound.

The riddle involving the bruises on Douglas Panton's body was never fully explained or investigated. Dr Miller believed the bruises had occurred before death, and most probably in a fall from the cliffs onto the rocks at Penlee Point. However, the majority of bruising was to the victim's forehead, with only minor bruising elsewhere. In addition, Dr Miller only mentioned one cut (to the eyelid) during his evidence at inquest. Surely, such a fall would have produced extensive and dramatic trauma to the entire body. The bruising and cut to the forehead appear to be more indicative of a blow to the skull, than a fall. In fact, Dr Miller also stated that it was equally likely that the bruising was, *'inflicted by a heavy fall, either by the falling of an object onto the body, or the body onto an object.'* The first part of his assessment here appears to have been ignored at the inquest, in favour of the last assumption.

Both men, were known to have been members of the Rhymers' Club, with similar interests in provocative literature, and both suffered from depression. Both men disappeared simultaneously, and both were known to be in Penzance on the probable day of their death. Douglas Panton (according to his ex-business partner Sidney Ellis) had never previously travelled to Cornwall, nor did he have any family there, or any known reason to visit. That these five factors should all align by pure coincidence seems highly improbable.

Part Three:

At the inquest into Douglas Panton's death, P.C. Whells was asked for his opinion as to the most likely cause of death. He stated that,

'I believe that the man took off his own clothes and donned the feminine garments on the cliff. He then walked to the highest point and put the handcuffs on

*his wrists and feet, intending to jump off into the sea,
but slipping accidentally, fell down the landward side
on to the rocks below.'*

Again, this seems highly improbable. How could a
person manacle his own limbs and then ensure that he
was able to hurl himself far enough from the cliff to
ensure that he landed in the sea and not merely hit the
rocks below. In addition, the steely resolve required for
such an endeavour can never be underestimated, nor
the natural human impulse to resist it. There are some
inconsistencies too with the injuries to Douglas
Panton's body. Although the victim's neck was
broken, there were no other broken limbs recorded.
Surely, such a violent fall would have created a number
of fractures and abrasions. After all, it would have been
impossible for Panton to have hurled himself from the
clifftop and then tied his limbs together at the bottom!
Although it is difficult to comprehend the mindset of
someone in such a traumatic emotional state, it
certainly seems unlikely that anyone would conjure up
such a painful, frightening, and lingering way to take
their own life.

Perhaps the two men undertook a macabre suicide pact
on that clifftop. Did Davidson help Panton manacle
himself, then either hit or push him over the edge, then
climb down to the beach and take his own life. Due to
the decomposition of Davidson's body after four
months in the water it was impossible to determine if
he too had suffered similar extensive bruising. The
inquest into Davidson's death was unable to confirm
exactly what happened, with any degree of certainty.

The most likely scenario appears to be, that a suicide pact took place on the rocky shoreline that day at Penlee Point. Davidson helped Panton secure his handcuffs, after the London solicitor had taken off his clothing, strewn them on the beach, and re-dressed in female attire. Davidson then assisted or half-dragged Panton out into the sea until Panton could no longer balance and Davidson could no longer hold his revolver above water. Davidson then pressed the gun to his forehead and pulled the trigger. Panton, the slighter of the two men, unable to use to arms or legs was then violently thrown against the rocks (causing the bruising and death), before being washed ashore and wedged between the rocks. Davidson's lifeless body then remained afloat long enough to drift out into the Sound where it was not recovered for nearly five months. Temporarily, his body may have possibly come to rest in a large rock pool at the mouth of a watery cave close to Mousehole, only to then wash out to sea once more - two young boys thought they had seen a body there a few days earlier. It was thought probable at Davidson's inquest, that his body may have been in the entrance to the cave for several months. However, it seems unlikely that a body would go unnoticed for five months in an area in which children played and fishermen regularly passed by. In any case, the high tides would almost certainly not have allowed a body to remain there indefinitely.

The possibility that the two men formed a joint suicide pact seems a more likely alternative; and does answer several troubling assumptions made at the two inquests. Firstly, if the events took place on the cliff top, why did nobody see Douglas Panton walking or changing clothes there? Secondly, why were his discarded man's clothes found on the beach and not on the cliffs above? Thirdly, the difficulty in ensuring the outcome he desired was far likelier to be achieved with the cooperation of another, than it was alone. Finally, no revolver was found either on the clifftop or shore (or, later, in the cave), seeming to indicate that John Davidson had probably already waded a considerable distance into the water before firing the fatal shot. Remember, his desire was to die and be buried at sea, not on land.

John Davidson left strict instructions that *'No biography of me should be written and none of my unpublished works published.'*

This leaves just one more puzzle in this tragic affair – Douglas Panton's decision to disguise himself as a woman. Perhaps he intended, with John Davidson's help, to remain missing and undiscovered for eternity; in a misguided assumption that his recovered body would never be identified as male. Maybe, in a more religious era of strict public morality he had lived a secret transgender life of shame, fuelled by his interest in illicit literature. This would certainly explain his family's failure to attend his funeral, and the fact that this aspect of his death was not considered suitable for both the public inquest and the newspaper coverage at the time.

Or, conceivably, his elaborate stunt was merely a snub at his family's artistic leanings, or a final theatrical gesture to a cruel world in which he clearly felt both a personal and financial failure.

The two fishermen who had discovered John Davidson's body collected the £20 reward. However, despite Douglas Panton's family's relative wealth, there is no record of any reward being offered in his case.

Scan here for extra photographs and digital versions of the images contained in this chapter

A History of Bedford
Row, London

Leaves From a Life by
Jane E. Panton

More about John
Davidson

The Poetry of John
Davidson

'Happy or unhappy, people disappear.'
Amanda Craig, A Vicious Circle

Part One:

There was a portentous atmosphere in London during April of 1913. The Suffragette activist Emmeline Pankhurst had just been sentenced to three years penal servitude for her part in the ongoing campaign for universal suffrage. Her imprisonment was soon followed with an arson attack by fellow supporters, which completely destroyed the cricket pavilion in Royal Tunbridge Wells – a symbol of the male establishment. Meanwhile, the 'Irish Problem' occupied the House of Commons, while further afield, the rumblings of militarisation could be heard from the continent.

Nevertheless, the ominous sound of impending war was not the most pressing consideration of most Londoners. The daily drudgery of poverty and overcrowding occupied the minds of most. According to a report by the Fabian Society, entitled *Round About a Pound a Week*, the reality of life among the 'respectable poor' meant one in five children dying within their first year, acute hunger, illness, and malnutrition. In London's East End an average of 25 houses shared one lavatory and one freshwater tap. The housing stock was outdated, outmoded, and in desperate need of improvement.

London, 1913

It was reported that as many as 20,000 people a year would mysteriously go missing in the capital city. Most were as a result of suicide, drunken accident, or a desperate attempt to escape debt and the misery of modern life. The void between rich and poor was a wide as ever.

Thankfully no such concerns played on the mind of wealthy American businessman John Joseph Wilberforce Martin, as he walked to the exclusive and palatial Royal Automobile Club (RAC) at 89 Pall Mall.

Mr J. J. W. Martin had been born in Memphis, Tennessee on 17th March 1871. After being educated in the finest public schools of Memphis, and then the University of Virginia, he had graduated with honours in 1891. Following university his family placed him in charge of the grocery department at Hill, Fontaine & Co. in Memphis. After a suitable introduction into the world of business he formed a partnership with William Phillips in 1900, under the name of Martin, Phillips & Co., cotton factors. The two men traded extensively and successfully throughout the United States and Europe.

Known to his acquaintances as simply Joseph, or Joe, Martin had been staying with his good friend Mr John Lockhart Anderson of 7 Park Place, just off St James's Street. Scottish by ancestry, and a long-term business associate of Martin's, Anderson had agreed to meet his American business associate at the prestigious Royal Automobile Club on the evening on Thursday 3rd April. Anderson had even arranged a temporary honorary RAC membership for Martin. They were to be joined for dinner by another colleague, Captain Prior of the Cavalry Club, followed by whisky, and cigars in the Great Gallery. The men then intended to finish the evening with a game of billiards,

As was traditional in the RAC Club, the three colleagues had all dressed for dinner. In addition, Martin was carrying his opera hat and at least £100 about his person in bank notes and gold sovereigns (an amount equivalent to approximately £13,000 today, or US $16,000). An appreciable sum of money with which to be walking the dimly lit streets of London in 1913.

The men spoke jovially of business and politics. Captain Prior was a man of independent means, and always on the lookout for a sound investment. Anderson was a partner in Bousfield and Anderson Merchants, of Mincing Lane in the city. Martin was a cotton broker and trader with a well-established business in his native Memphis, and an extensive network of contacts throughout Tennessee and Arkansas. In recent years his business dealings had seen him expand as an exporter into Europe and the British Empire. With increases in spending on military uniforms and equipment expected by all the major European governments, he had travelled to London to broker a large cotton transaction. From a well-known and highly respected Tennessee family, Joseph Wilberforce Martin was reported by the London Stock Exchange to be worth at least £200,000 (equivalent to some £25 million, or $30 million, today). Indeed, it had been rumoured on the floor of the Stock Exchange, that Martin's net worth had risen by further £10,000 during recent days. He had seemingly struck a business deal since arriving in London, for the sale of options on several large US cotton plantations.

Captain Prior and John Lockhart Anderson were somewhat surprised when Martin called an abrupt end to the evening around 11pm. He had booked a return passage to the United States aboard the CGT liner *La France* and was due to leave on Saturday morning. The three men shook hands and promised to meet again at the club the following evening, Friday 4th April, which would be Martin's final night in London before sailing. When asked by his colleagues why he wished to leave the club earlier than planned that night, Martin announced that he had an appointment with *'a beautiful and dark Brazilian lady.'*

Prior and Anderson escorted their friend to the door of the club and stood at the imposing entrance while Martin hailed a taxi. At 11.10pm, Anderson and Prior waved as Martin climbed into the taxicab, which then headed along Pall Mall in a westward direction towards Green Park. They had the strong impression that the taxicab then turned right into St James's Street (the London address of John Lockhart Anderson), however, the night was dark, and the turning some 250 yards away, making it difficult for either man to be certain in which direction the taxicab had gone among the hubbub of traffic in Pall Mall.

The two men were slightly surprised by Martin's sudden exit, and his rather out of character announcement regarding an assignation with a *'beautiful and dark Brazilian lady'*. However, as Martin had already promised to meet both men again on the following evening at the club, they were not unduly alarmed. It would be Martin's final night before sailing for New York and he had assured his friends, *'it will be a leaving party to remember!'*

John Anderson and Captain Prior met punctually at the R.A.C. Club the following evening (Friday 4th April 1913), however there was no sign of Joseph Wilberforce Martin. They duly waited, expecting him to be a little late, as was his custom. However, as the minutes turned to hours, the two men became more and more concerned.

Eventually the two anxious friends, tired of waiting, hailed the RAC's telegram boy and wired several messages to various London clubs, hotels, and houses that Martin may have possibly visited. This produced no results. Anderson then remembered that Martin occasionally suffered from fits. Perhaps he had collapsed somewhere following a seizure, they surmised, and had been taken to a hospital where he had not yet been revived. They immediately wired telegrams to several London hospitals, but all to no avail. Perhaps, he was merely resting somewhere quietly until the effects of the seizures had worn off, Captain Prior suggested. However, they could find no evidence of this, and the two friends began to grow increasing uneasy. They decided to contact Vine Street police station, who in turn referred the case to Scotland Yard. Due to the wealth and profile of the rich American, Detective Chief Inspector Ward, and a handpicked band of experienced C.I.D. officers, were despatched to investigate. They immediately questioned John Lockhart Anderson and Captain Prior. Martin's two acquaintances confirmed that they had witnessed their friend climbing into a taxicab at 11.10pm on Thursday evening. He had been smartly dressed, with no luggage, and carrying an opera hat, they confirmed.

Knowing that Martin had intended to board the *La France* that morning, the police hastily wired the London ticket office of Compagnie Générale Transatlantique, only to find that the ship had already departed. The ticket office was able to confirm that, as far as they were aware, Mr Martin had not boarded the American bound liner, neither had he cancelled his passage. With the advent of the new Marconi wireless system an urgent morse code message was relayed to the *La France* as it sped towards the New World. A check was made of Mr Martin's compartment onboard, which was empty and untouched. It seems that he had not boarded the *La France*, or at any rate, not under his own name.

The *La France* was considered an unlucky ship by many who sailed on her. She had been introduced on the North Atlantic routes just one week after the sinking of the *Titanic*, just twelve months earlier, an event still painfully raw in the minds of the British public. Her four funnels and other similarities in appearance to the ill-fated *Titanic*, gave her a somewhat poignant appearance. Perhaps the *La France* had been an unlucky omen for Joseph Wilberforce Martin?

Next, detectives visited the suite of rooms at 7 Park Place, the mansion belonging to John Lockhart Anderson, in which Martin had been staying during his business trip to London. Despite the two witnesses believing that Martin's taxicab had turned into Park Place on the night of his disappearance, Martin's luggage was still inside the bedroom, untouched, and ready for his voyage, right down to the intact shipping labels marked '*La France – New York*'. It had not been disturbed since Martin had left the room at some point during the previous evening, on his way to meet his colleagues at the RAC Club. Although there was no cash present, all of Martin's jewellery, a small strongbox, a valuable gold dress watch, and his private papers were all still inside the room. These papers included some important documentation relating to a business transaction for £10,000, apparently his primary reason for visiting London. His cheque book and deposit book, together with his other banking credentials were also present. From the details on his cheque book, the police officers were able to verify with the London and Westminster Bank that Martin's account had not been touched since a sum of money had been withdrawn on Thursday morning. This sum probably accounted for at least part of the £100 Martin was known to have had on his person at the time of his disappearance. Despite now being missing for more than 24 hours, neither Martin nor anyone pretending to be him had attempted to withdraw any further funds from his account. It seemed an ominous sign to the investigating officers.

Now missing for more than 36 hours, with no sightings of Martin, Chief Inspector Dark seemed perplexed. After all, to go missing is not a crime, yet there seemed to be no logical reason for Joseph Martin to voluntarily vanish from sight. Perhaps the American millionaire had merely wished to hide from public scrutiny for a short while; and would resurface sheepishly in a month or two? However, Martin's colleague John Anderson pressed the police, insisting that *'his disappearance is so utterly out of character that sinister forces must have been in play.'*

Amid a blaze of publicity, the police assigned an additional three detectives to the investigation and quickly concluded that they were left with three possible plans of action. Firstly, rely on the media and general public by issuing a description of the missing man. Secondly, attempt to trace the mysterious and exotic Brazilian lady; and thirdly, begin a search of hospitals, alleyways, and perhaps even the River Thames, for the victim of a robbery and murder.

One of the investigating officers, Detective Sergeant Smith, thought it likely that Martin had taken a ferry or boat to the continent, despite the crew of the *La France* being convinced that he was not onboard. The liner had been scheduled to call at Le Havre in France before steaming for New York. Perhaps Martin had simply disembarked there; and had no intention of returning to the States at all? It was decided to simultaneously wire his description to all European ports and railway stations, together with the missing persons bureaus of the Paris, Brussels, and Berlin police forces. Several British newspapers, post offices, and banks were also issued with the following description:

'The missing man is an American bachelor, aged 41; complexion fair. Hair, fair, turning grey. Very high forehead; wears glasses. Height 5ft. 4ins. When last seen was wearing evening (dinner) jacket with velvet collar, a black overcoat, and a very valuable gold dress watch.'

Joseph Martin

A public appeal for information was initiated, in an attempt to establish the identity and location of the enigmatic Brazilian beauty, of whom Martin had boasted indiscreetly to his friends. Enquiries were made at several London hotels, known to be frequented by visitors from South America, and at the Brazilian embassy in Green Street, Mayfair. However, despite their extensive efforts, no suitable name was given to Scotland Yard and no individual came forward to identify themself as the shadowy lady.

From that point onward, the emphasis of the investigation switched from that of an unexplained disappearance, to one of robbery and possible murder, when a startling discovery was made on the other side of the River Thames. Although the discovery was initially made on the morning following Martin's disappearance, it was not reported to the police until several days later. Early on the morning of Friday 4th April. Mr George Barnes, a labourer, was walking to work along Belvedere Road on the south bank of the Thames, when he noticed a discarded opera hat and man's pocketbook lying behind some railings in the yard of Eastwood and Co, Brick Merchants, close to the railway line and a few feet from the slope leading to Hungerford Bridge, which cast its shadow over the road below.

George Barnes initially attached no importance to his find which lay on the mantelpiece at his home for several days before he eventually contacted the police. Having seen the description of Mr Martin in the London newspapers, Mr Barnes contacted Scotland Yard. The pocketbook carried the monogram *'J.W.M.'*, making it almost certainly the missing millionaire's. Chief Inspector Dark and Sergeant Smith visited Mr Barnes at his home.

A detailed description of the pocketbook's contents was recorded in Chief Inspector Dark's notebook, in the hope it might yield a vital clue,

'The pocketbook which was of dark Morocco leather is inscribed with the initials "J. W. M.". It contained: An old Cunard Line passage ticket from New York in Mr. Martin's name. Receipt for 12s. 6d. from a safe deposit company in Cannon Street. A dozen private visiting cards inscribed "J.W. Martin, Memphis, Tenn.", a dozen business cards, bearing the inscription "J.W. Martin cotton factor". A Savoy Hotel card. A temporary honorary membership card of the Royal Automobile Club with the name of Mr. Martin's friend. Mr. J. Lockhart Anderson, with whom he dined on April 3, as nominator. A card bearing the name of a West End doctor. The pocketbook has three compartments, one being fastened by a button. This compartment was ripped open as though it had been torn in a hurry and was empty. The other compartment was also empty.'

The officers had been informed by Mr Martin's friends that the American was in the habit of carrying a small personal diary inside his pocketbook, in which he noted his engagements and appointments. Unfortunately, the diary in question was missing. It had been hoped that it might contain the name, time, and place of his mysterious appointment with the '*dark and beautiful*' lady from Brazil.

Nevertheless, Mr Barnes was also able to tell the detectives about an opera hat he had seen lying next to the discarded wallet. The detectives then asked Mr Barnes to accompany them to Belvedere Road and point out the exact location at which he had first noticed these two crucial pieces of evidence.

Meanwhile, a 15-year-old lad named Harold Salter, while walking to work at the Lion Brewery in Belvedere Road, had spotted the opera hat lying on the side of the road on Friday 4th April, the day after Mr Martin's disappearance. The boy, who was late for work, had initially left the hat, but decided to go back afterwards and collect it. He noticed a $4^{1/2}$-inch gold chain lodged inside the lining of the hat. The chain was fitted with a stud at one end, used to secure a gentleman's pocketbook to his buttonhole (Mr Martin was known to favour wearing such a stud and chain). Unfortunately, the young lad, together with his friends, had decided to use the opera hat as a football, during which time the gold chain had been lost and the hat badly damaged. When the description of Mr Martin had been circulated Harold Salter's father clipped his son around the ear and instructed him to take the opera hat to the police immediately. Although the hat yielded no further clues for the police, and was not monogrammed, it almost certainly had belonged to the missing millionaire.

Part Two:

The theory that Mr Martin had been robbed and then murdered gained momentum. However, how did his pocketbook and opera hat find their way across the river to Belvedere Road? Was Mr Martin travelling in that direction, or was he lured there, perhaps by the lady from Brazil, of whom there was still no trace? The items were certainly already in Belvedere Road by 5.30am the following morning (when first noticed by George Barnes). This seemed to suggest that Mr

Martin had most probably been in that vicinity not long after leaving his friends at the RAC Club in Pall Mall. It was a journey of less than two miles and could be walked without difficulty in twenty minutes or so. By taxicab it was a short ten-minute drive away, past the House of Commons and across Westminster Bridge. Chief Inspector Dark had his suspicions and gave a statement to the reporters gathered outside 4 Whitehall Place, the entrance to Scotland Yard Police Headquarters, revealing that he had, in fact, previously met Joseph Martin:

'I often used to see Mr Joseph Martin, the missing American millionaire. He was popular in the West End and well known in the City. I believe that Mr Martin, was lured in by a gang of three desperadoes or anarchists, possibly in the Kennington area of London, drugged and robbed, and then being passed off as being simply another man the worse for drink (resulting from his drugged condition), *taken to the river and thrown in. The hat and the wallet, I think, were purposely left in Belvedere Road.'*

The police officer's theory regarding the position of the hat and wallet seemed to concur with the opinion of Mr Barnes and the young lad, Harold Salter, who were both of the strong opinion that the items had been deliberately 'staged' to send the police in the wrong direction, perhaps searching buildings and yards close to Belvedere Road, instead of concentrating their efforts around the riverbank.

Belvedere Road

Yet, as the days passed, the oddity of this location puzzled Chief Inspector Dark. Despite an asserted search effort by the River Police alongside the flowing banks of the Thames, if Mr Martin had indeed been robbed and murdered, the body had yet to be discovered. A corpse dumped in the river would normally have been expected to float to the surface within a couple of days. Had it simply been washed out to sea without a trace? However, if Mr Martin had simply wished to vanish quietly for a short period, why go to such lengths to conceal his true location or intentions? And, if the real objective had always been to simply throw Mr Martin's body in the river, why not just dispose of the pocketbook and opera hat in the same way?

Conceivably, Mr Martin had intended to disappear after all? Yet, surely, the staged discarding of his pocketbook and hat was too simple a ruse. If Martin had really wished to maintain a low profile, then surely, allowing himself to be witnessed wandering the South Bank in full evening dress in the middle of the night would have attracted comment and attention? Or had someone else carefully planted the pocketbook and hat on Martin's behalf, which raised the question of the Brazilian lady once more.

It is perhaps not surprising that Chief Inspector Dark erred on the side of pessimism in reaching his conclusions, even without a great deal in the way of evidence to substantiate his fears. London at that time was a violent and volatile city. Several anarchist (what might now be called terrorist) groups were operating within the city. Murder and robbery were commonplace; and numerous criminal gangs governed large swathes of the capital, demanding money with menaces.

On the day that Martin's opera hat was recovered, Scotland Yard also dealt with a £50,000 diamond robbery at the home of the French ambassador, two plots involving German nationals, including a gunpowder bomb in a milk pail placed at the entrance to the Bank of England, a bank robbery linked to a notorious London gang, three murders, and a case of kidnap and blackmail – not to mention fifty further missing persons reports filed at the various London police stations. Coupled with the unenviable reputation of the district surrounding Belvedere Road, it is perhaps not surprising, that Chief Inspector Dark feared the worst.

Ten days had now passed since Joseph Martin's disappearance and there had been little movement on the case. No trace had been found of the Brazilian lady, nor of the taxicab driver who had collected Mr Martin from outside the RAC Club on the previous Thursday evening. The police were extremely puzzled that neither of these two individuals had come forward voluntarily, assuming they had nothing to hide. In fact, were it not for the evidence of Mr J. Lockhart Anderson and Captain Prior, the police might have been forgiven for thinking that both were merely a figment of the imagination.

Public fascination with the story quickly reached fever pitch. The Edwardian era has been called 'the golden era of detective fiction', and the public – fuelled by lurid newspaper speculation - soon responded with sightings and solutions of their own. It seemed that Joseph Wilberforce Martin was very much alive in the imagination of London's residents.

Meanwhile, the Martin family in Memphis had been contacted and the awful news relayed to them. They wasted no time in attempting to assist the investigation. Mr Fontaine Martin and Mrs Eugenia Bridger, Joseph

Martin's younger brother and sister, announced a reward of £500 (£63,000 today) for any information resulting in the discovery of the missing man's whereabouts.

THE MISSING MILLIONAIRE.

Mr. Joseph Wilberforce Martin, the American millionaire, who has been missing in London since Thursday week.

They employed the services of New York based William J. Burns; the famous private investigator known as 'the American Sherlock Holmes'. Burns had already been involved in several high-profile cases through the agency he had founded, The William J. Burns International Detective Agency. He would also later become Director of the Bureau of Investigation (the forerunner to the F.B.I.). Even today, his legacy survives. The Burns Agency was absorbed into Securitas Security Services USA, an international security and detection firm with over 300,000 employees worldwide.

The Martin family paid William J. Burn's passage across the Atlantic and for his accommodation at the Savoy Hotel in the centre of London. From here, he began his own private investigation into the disappearance of Joseph Martin – much to the chagrin of Scotland Yard. A large group of newspapermen gathered outside the Savoy Hotel, hoping for a glimpse of the famous American detective, and for an exclusive scope on the story. William J. Burn's, a master of the shrewd soundbite, informed the amassed reporters, *'I am confident that Mr Martin is alive and in London at the present time.'*

Chief Inspector Ward at Scotland Yard was also questioned by the newshounds from Fleet Street, although rather than being asked about the ongoing investigations, it seemed that the gathered reporters were more interested in the friction between the two great detectives,

'Tell me Chief Inspector', asked one reporter, *'might Mr Burns find Mr Martin before Scotland Yard does?'*

'He might,' the Chief Inspector begrudgingly admitted, *'if we at Scotland Yard do not get Martin*

first. The trail is getting warmer all the time, and it is now a certainty that the man is alive and in the city.'

'So, Chief Inspector, are the rumours of sightings true?'

William J Burns

'We believe that we have traced Mr Martin and the persons who are holding him to a certain house in

Kennington yesterday afternoon. But when we arrived there the birds had flown, evidently fearing a trap. However, they did not fly far, and we are now hot on their tracks.'

Meanwhile, it was soon determined by William J. Burns that a Brazilian lady matching the description of the woman sought by police, had boarded the liner *Kaiser Wilhelm II* bound for New York. With little information to go on, and carrying no identification to determine her nationality, the police were unable to detain the lady before her departure from Southampton. However, they hoped to wire the port authorities in New York and request that she be questioned there. The mysterious lady was described by fellow passengers as *'Creole'* in appearance, tall and glamorous, and using the nickname *'Baby Ruth'*. She had booked her passage under the much less exotic name 'Mrs Morris Maloney', and managed to somehow avoid being questioned upon her arrival in the US; whereupon she promptly vanished.

Meanwhile, Joseph Martin's brother and nephew booked passage on the Cunard liner *Campania* and vowed to travel to London to assist in the search. However, the two siblings seem to have quickly changed their minds concerning travelling across the Atlantic. There appear to have been a number of factors which caused their sudden change of heart. Firstly, William J. Burns (perhaps preferring to work alone on the case) cabled Fontaine Martin as follows:

'Your presence in London unnecessary. Your brother will be found within a day or two.- W.J.B.'

It also emerged that Fontaine Martin had received a last-minute telegram from his mother, Nina Martin, begging him not to travel to London in the search of her other son. Fontaine Martin (already having journeyed as far as New York) cancelled his passage aboard the *Campania*, took a taxicab to Pennsylvania Station in Midtown Manhattan, and boarded the 'Memphis Special'. He arrived in Tennessee at 8am the following morning, where he spoke to waiting reporters,

'This thing is breaking my mother's heart. I'm afraid it's killing her. I have to go back home, that's all.'

In the meantime, Mr Anderson had been tirelessly engaged in the quest for his friend Joseph Martin. On the morning of Friday 11th April, eight days after his friend's disappearance, Mr Anderson announced that he was offering a reward of his own for information leading to the discovery of Joseph Martin.

His announcement, issued via the London News Agency, was made at the culmination of a difficult week for Mr Anderson. Rumours that he had somehow been involved in the mystery had circulated among members of the press. There had been speculation of a business deal gone wrong, that Martin had reneged on a financial promise, a defaulted loan, and even of a potential fraud.

'I am offered a reward of £100 for any information leading to the discovery of my good friend and business acquaintance Mr Joseph Wilberforce Martin,' announced Mr Anderson, *'not only have I told the authorities investigating the disappearance*

everything I know in connection with the case, but I have already spent nearly £1,000 ($5,000) *out of my own pocket in an endeavour to get Mr Martin back. He and I were putting together a big cotton deal, which, according to Martin, promised to net us something like £1,000,000 profit. Mr Martin's disappearance has upset the deal, so you can see how anxious I am to find him.'*

This figure was a staggering amount in 1913, today's equivalent of at least £123 million (or $150 million). However, rather than assuage the public's opinion that John Anderson may have been involved in his friend's disappearance, the revelation seemed to have had the opposite effect. Anderson appeared to be under huge strain and made several visits to his physician during the weeks that followed Martin's disappearance. He was also summoned to Scotland Yard to be interviewed by Sir Melville Macnaghten, the Assistant Commissioner of the Metropolitan Police. A popular and influential figure, Sir Melville no doubt wished to gain his own perspective on the case. Similarly to Chief Inspector Dark, Sir Melville had also worked on the Whitechapel Murders and the case of Dr Crippen. In fact, he claimed to know the real identity of Jack the Ripper but had always refused to reveal the truth, stating that the killer had taken his own life shortly after the final killing. Nevertheless, Sir Melville was no longer at the height of his powers by 1913. He was already in poor health and had been so for several years. He retired shortly after his involvement in the Joseph Martin case and does not appear to have been able to add anything to the investigation. He died in

1921 without ever having publicly revealed the identity of the Whitechapel murderer.

Sir Melville Macnaghten

Nevertheless, the search for Joseph Martin continued unabated. Other rewards were added by several individuals and newspapers until the amount available for the discovery of the missing millionaire's location reached an eye-catching £1,100. Many Fleet Street newspapers, joined by their American colleagues, carried advertisements imploring the public to pass on any important leads in the case.

Perhaps surprisingly, Scotland Yard did not welcome the announcement of potential riches for anyone coming forward with useful information. They did not publicly mention the rewards in any interview or formal statements given to the press. The reason was possibly twofold. Firstly, some negative press speculation had emphasised the more pedestrian efforts of Scotland Yard, compared with the energy shown by William J. Burns. The official force certainly had no wish to highlight this point. In fact, one newspaper had even instigated a campaign to persuade the respected Walter Dew out of retirement to solve the case.

Walter Dew

Dew had retired from Scotland Yard in 1910, after having made his name in the high-profile investigations such as the case of the Russian fraudster Friedlauski, the Whitechapel Murders, and the arrest of Dr Crippen. Walter Dew had famously boarded the *SS Montrose* as she steamed into the St Lawrence River on the US Canadian border, having first climbed aboard disguised as a river pilot. He then removed his pilot's cap and said, *"Good morning, Dr Crippen. Do you know me? I'm Chief Inspector Dew from Scotland Yard."* The incident had assured lifelong fame for Dew but, despite being consulted, he too could not help his colleagues with Joseph Martin's mysterious disappearance.

Secondly, Scotland Yard may have feared that the announcement of a large reward would merely lead to a bombardment of red herrings and far-fetched 'clues' from the public, all of which would tie up valuable police resources at a crucial point in the investigation. This proved to be the case.

The owner and manager of a small hotel in Victoria Street contacted Scotland Yard on Saturday 12th April, convinced that a lone American staying at the hotel was the missing millionaire. The man's appearance was similar to the description of Mr Martin recently featured in the London press. It seems the furtive gentleman had been a guest at the hotel since 8th April and was not due to leave for another week, Regrettably, when the police arrived, the American guest had mysteriously checked out just an hour before the arrival of detectives, informing the hotel clerk that he was *'unhappy with a charge on his account and would be checking into another hotel around the block.'*. All the hotel manager could add, was, *'I noticed yesterday that the gentleman drove up to the hotel accompanied by a fashionably dressed lady, another gentleman, and a chauffeur. He had a somewhat strange manner and an accent.'*

The police were unable to trace this mysterious lone American at any of the nearby hotels.

Perhaps Mr Martin was receiving some help, or perhaps the mysterious hotel guest was completely unrelated to the mystery? We will never know. However, this important clue did tally with the statement of a taxicab driver who came forward on the same day. He claimed to have picked up a fare from outside the Royal Automobile Club, around 11pm on Thursday 3rd April, and dropped him at a Victoria Street hotel. Unfortunately, the taxi driver could not remember the man's face, although he did remember that his passenger had an American accent and that the American had asked to stop off in Trafalgar Square, on their way to the hotel, to pick up a well-dressed lady.

The Royal Automobile Club, Pall Mall

In a separate line of enquiry, a landlord from Shephard's Bush reported that Mr Martin had rented a tiny room in a rundown dwelling in Devonport Road. It may have been the perfect cover for a millionaire wishing to hide away. However, he would have appeared conspicuous to say the least. With no real evidence to support the landlord's claim, the police quickly dismissed this line of enquiry.

A clairvoyant claimed to be haunted by a vision of Mr Martin, being held illegally, in a house somewhere off the Waterloo Road. The mystic believed that the missing millionaire had been imprisoned by a desperate group of kidnappers, who were holding him against his will while they plotted their ransom demand. No demand had yet been forthcoming; and the police politely dismissed the clairvoyant.

Another odd rumour reached the desk of Scotland Yard in the weeks following Martin's disappearance, this time from an official at Southampton Docks. He swore to the police that he had witnessed Martin on the evening of Friday 4th April (the night after he had vanished from the steps of the R.A.C. Club) boarding the Union Castle liner *Walmer Castle* at the Royal Pier, bound for the Cape Colonies. The official told police that the man was wearing *'evening dress and a slouch hat'*. This piqued Chief Inspector's Dark interest, who then wired the vessel. However, several days had passed since the ship's departure and there was no record of a man resembling Joseph Martin onboard. Realistically, it would have been easy for the mystery passenger to have disembarked at one of several ports while enroute to the Cape.

Many were convinced that the missing cotton broker had become entangled with a group of hardened gamblers during his stay in London. His friend, John Anderson, confirmed to the police that Martin enjoyed a game of cards and would frequently bet large sums. Conceivably a pressing debt may have been called in, or perhaps Martin had fleeced one of the many London criminal gangs known to be involved in the numerous gambling dens dotted around the capital city. It was certainly considered a distinct possibility that one of these gangs may have been holding Martin against his will.

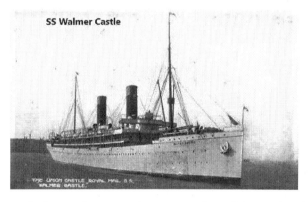
SS Walmer Castle

Nevertheless, these various strands of investigation presented detectives with little in the way of fresh evidence and the trail seemed to be growing ever colder. However, this was to change significantly on Wednesday 16th April 1913, when a mysterious advertisement appeared in the personal column of several London newspapers. The listing read simply:

'Essential you should communicate with your brothers.'

It is difficult today to realise the importance of newspaper personal columns during the Victorian and Edwardian eras. Secret plots, illicit love affairs, and criminal activities all played out on a daily basis in such columns – all in plain sight. Use of these listings allowed parties to communicate openly, without fear of others understanding their coded messages. The newspaper reading public were well aware, however, and hours of fun could be enjoyed attempting to decipher the possible meanings hidden behind the words. This particular message seemed to convince many that Joseph Martin was still very much alive.

Meanwhile, on the same day a telegram reached Captain Prior at Royal Automobile Club. Cabled from Vevey, a small town on Lake Geneva in Switzerland, the message simply stated:

'Perfectly safe. Cease search. Letter follows. - Joe Martin.'

No letter ever did follow. Nevertheless, acting on this information, Scotland Yard communicated with the Swiss Police in Vevey, however no trace could be found of the missing millionaire. The staff at the Vevey Post Office could not recall the sender, so the author of the telegram remained a mystery. Conceivably Joseph Martin had intended to disappear and had arranged for an acquaintance in Vevey to send the telegram, perhaps in an attempt to save his family some anguish? The telegram seemed to convince William J. Burns, who returned to the United States shortly afterwards, stating, *'I consider the case now closed. All interest ceases for me now that we know Martin is alive and well.'*

He may have been too hasty.

A similar message was also sent to the London Evening Standard, and read as follows:

'My friend Mr Martin safe and well. – Anderson'

Initially, it appeared that the message had originated from Mr Martin's colleague J. Lockhart Anderson. However, detectives were able to trace the source of this message, as having originated from the telegraph desk at Westminster Bridge Post Office. The telegram had been written by a woman, and a sample of the lady's handwriting from the original telegram request form was kept at Scotland Yard in case it could ever be matched to a suspect. It never was.

Meanwhile, an interesting development unfolded in the investigation. Not in London, but more than four-thousand miles away, across the Atlantic in Memphis.

Mr Fontaine Martin, Joseph Martin's brother, announced that the family business, the Martins Phillips Company, had filed for bankruptcy in the Federal Courts. The liabilities of the firm were listed as $430,140 and its assets as $403,163. The company was technically solvent – to the tune of $23. However, the majority of the firm's assets were tied up in commodities – mainly bales of cotton in its Tennessee warehouse. It would soon be revealed that Joseph Martin had obtained a substantial loan from an American bank using the company's 1,800 bales of cotton as collateral. With cotton prices currently increasing to approximately $60 per bale (a bale consisted of 495lbs of cotton), and with increased spending on army uniforms and equipment by Europe's governments, the bales seemed a sound security investment for the bank. However, an inventory check of the company's warehouse had identified that only 94 bales were actually stored there. The company produced invoices and receipts, signed by the warehouse manager, which seemed to indicate that 1,800 bales of cotton had been legitimately purchased by the company and were stored in their warehouse. However, the warehouse manager claimed to have no knowledge of the transactions and denied that the signature on the dockets was his. Perhaps the real reason for Joseph Martin's disappearance was beginning to surface.

Mr Fontaine Martin also revealed the supposed purpose of his brother's visit to London. Just hours before his disappearance from the RAC Club in Pall Mall on 3rd April, Joseph Martin had apparently cabled his brother in Memphis. Mr Fontaine Martin divulged the facts to the American press,

'My brother, Mr Joseph Martin, had, on April 3rd, closed a deal involving the sale of 60,000 acres of cotton land in Arkansas and Tennessee, valued at more than $100 an acre, to an English syndicate. I understand that the deal was made through my brother's London agent, Bousfield and Anderson, a broking and banking firm. That night, Joe disappeared. Since that moment, Mr J. Lockhart Anderson has been the family's only source of information regarding my brother's disappearance. Anderson has sent us absolutely nothing concerning the several millions which I believe must have changed hands to close the land sale. Joe was no rube! (American slang for a country bumpkin or simpleton). *Anderson has cabled us all the events of Joe's disappearance; but has avoided all mention of the money my brother is supposed to have received for his*

lands. When I get to London, Anderson will have to do business with me in a hurry!'

Two months later in June 1913 Mr Fontaine Martin also revealed that, *'prior to Joe's disappearance, I had previously loaned my brother around $50,000 to assist with his cashflow problems.'*

This seemed to confirm in the minds of the police, the newspapers, and the private detective William J. Burns, that Joseph Martin had every reason to vanish so suddenly. The theory that he may have been robbed and murdered now seemed less likely.

Although the police officially kept the case file open in the quest for Mr Martin, a final series of handwritten notes, written by Chief Inspector Dark in the latter part of 1913, seemed to conclude the authorities' interest in the affair.

'SEVEN THEORIES:-

At least seven different theories are entered in these notes, these being:
- That Mr. Martin was decoyed to the spot, killed, and his body thrown into the Thames.
- That he was attacked and seriously injured and is lying ill at some house.
- That he is suffered a mental breakdown and has lost his memory.
- That the hat and pocketbook were thrown from a passing train.
- That Mr. Martin has deliberately disappeared from his friends for personal reasons.
- That he has been kidnapped.

– That a thief might well have taken the pocketbook to the spot in Belvedere Road to open it, where he was not likely to be seen, and that the discovery of the hat and the pocketbook in that same spot seems to point to a struggle and to foul play.'

Interestingly, the idea that Martin's colleague Mr Anderson was involved in the disappearance (a theory so popular among the press and public), does not seem to have been seriously entertained by the police. Although the rather intriguing possibility that the empty pocketbook and hat were merely tossed from a passing train does seem to warrant more investigation than it appears to have been given by Scotland Yard.

The pocketbook and hat were discovered adjacent to the spiked iron railings, at the gateway into the yard of Messrs Eastwood & Company, below the slope at the beginning of the Hungerford Bridge. Any pedestrian wishing to gain access by foot to the spot where the items were found, would have needed to walk a further 50 yards southwards, then turn right at the point where the Hungerford Bridge spans the road, about 40 feet above pavement level. However, anyone travelling in a train over the bridge would have found the task of throwing the opera hat and pocketbook into Messrs Eastwood & Company's yard below, a relatively easy one. The carriage windows of any passing train were comfortably higher than the iron sides of the Hungerford Bridge, giving the discarded items an unencumbered journey from an open window to ground level below. Perhaps this important point might account for the fact that the gold chain was still inside the opera hat when it was first discovered. The gold chain and pocketbook may have simply been placed inside the opera hat for ease, before tossing the hat from the carriage window. Conceivably, in fact, if Joseph Martin did throw the items from the train, perhaps he had intended them to land in the River Thames and not on land at all, thus helping to cover his tracks? Remember, it would have been extremely dark, there was only a waning crescent moon that night, and Martin was unfamiliar with the city.

In 1913, no less than twenty-two trains each day passed over Hungerford Bridge between 11.10pm (the time Martin was seen leaving the Royal Automobile Club), and 5.30am (when the discarded items were first spotted). Unfortunately, this avenue of enquiry does not appear to have been fully explored, leaving the intriguing question of Joseph Martin's intended destination or motives unanswered (coincidentally, a similar thread was followed by detectives in one of the later chapters in this book).

Slowly but surely, the separate lines of investigation dried up. The police were unable to trace the enigmatic Brazilian lady. Apart from the vague evidence of one taxicab driver, there had been no confirmed sightings of the missing man. A shopkeeper who came forward, claimed to have given directions to a well-dressed gentleman in Wandsworth, in the small hours of 4th April. However, he was unable to confirm that the man was Joseph Martin from the photographs provided to him by detectives.

The Martin's family business in Memphis was rescued from bankruptcy and scandal by Joseph Martin's brother Fontaine, and his wealthy grandfather William

M. Wood. Ultimately, the search for the missing millionaire seemed to result in more questions than answers. If Mr Martin had really been robbed and murdered, then no remains were ever found, nor was any likely culprit ever apprehended. On the other hand, if he had simply disappeared; then he did so without leaving a single clue to his whereabouts – a remarkably difficult undertaking to achieve. Martin's bank account remained untouched, nor did he ever return to the rooms at 7 Park Place for the money, jewellery, and strongbox he had left behind.

Tired of the inertia in the investigation, the British public soon lost interest in the search for Joseph Martin. By the end of 1913 the detectives on the case had been reassigned, and Sir Melville Macnaghten had retired. The early release of Emmeline Pankhurst from prison and the gloomy news from the continent now occupied the public's attentions. Intimidating proclamations of German power, in the form of vast dirigibles and mighty warships loomed across the channel. Within twelve months Britain would be at war. Four long years followed, in which many millions lost their lives. Almost as soon as the Great War had finished, the scourge of the 'Spanish Flu' pandemic killed millions more around the world. Then came some relief in the 'roaring twenties' before the stock market crash and the reality of the Great Depression touched the lives of almost everyone. The name of Joseph Martin had long been forgotten.

Part Three:

In the meantime, the Martin family's Memphis-based cotton business, the Martins Phillips Company, restructured and reorganised, and survived the loss of its managing partner. After being besieged by creditors in 1913, the company managed to repay its outstanding debts; propped up by private family money, and the rise in commodity prices which had been fuelled by the increase in military spending between 1914-18. The Martins managed to escape any retribution for their alleged loan fraud. With Joseph Martin listed as *'officially missing presumed dead'*, and with no further clues, there seemed little more the authorities could do. The case file remained technically open, although no further investigative work was undertaken by the police.

Despite loaning his brother £50,000 in 1913, Fontaine Martin does not seem to have been unduly financially embarrassed. In 1916 he purchased the Fox Plantation estate, just outside Memphis, for $45,000 (approximately $1.2 million today). In the years that followed the Great War an infestation of Boll Weevil affected a large number of cotton plantations in the southern states, forcing the cotton workers to migrate to other states, or to cities in the north, in an attempt to find work. This *'negro exodus'* - as it was labelled in the southern press at the time - left many of the plantation owners *'negro-bereft'*, and greatly affected Fontaine Martin, who had lost three-quarters of his cotton workers during 1923. He was forced to switch to corn and hay production for a time, before eventually selling his interests. In the years that followed, he maintained a lower public profile and largely slipped from view, choosing to concentrate his energies on golf and racehorse ownership instead. His horse, 'Nina Direct', named after his mother, was a regular entrant in harness races at Tri-State fairs and racetracks throughout the south.

Mr J. Lockhart Anderson did likewise. After the Great War his trading firm, Bousfield and Anderson, used their London connections to run a series of lucrative auctions, selling cotton, silks, and other raw materials in various parts of the country. Following the high-profile disappearance of Joseph Martin in 1913, Anderson also seems to have shied away from the headlines (and from the capital city).

From this point, the hunt for the missing Memphis millionaire ground to a halt. *The Times Despatch*, in Richmond, Virginia, called the story '*A Nine-Day Wonder'*. The sizeable police operation, which had involved a huge number of officers, contacting scores of hotels, hospitals, and gentleman's clubs, and questioning large numbers of potential witnesses, ultimately proved fruitless. A reward of more than £1,000 had failed to locate even the taxicab driver or the beautiful Brazilian lady. Dragging the River Thames for a body had yielded nothing. No further clues materialised. Even Scotland Yard's leading detectives could not locate Joseph Martin.

The telegram wired from Switzerland had convinced William J. Burns that Martin was alive, and he consequently returned to America, Sir Melville Macnaghten had retired, and even the Martin family eventually ceased their efforts to locate their sibling.

John Joseph Wilberforce Martin had stepped into a taxicab in Pall Mall at 11.10pm on the night of 3rd April 1913, never to be seen again.

And so, there ended the story of the missing millionaire. The search had petered out in a disappointing anti-climax and Joseph Martin had seemingly vanished from the face of the earth. Until, that is, one July day seventeen years later.

By 1930 the world had changed dramatically from the carefree days of the roaring twenties. The world's economy was spiralling into the Great Depression following the stock market crashes of 1929. More than 1,000 US banks would collapse before the end of the year. Politicians had begun to clamour for protectionism in a desperate attempt to prevent the further loss of American jobs, and against the threat of cheaper imports. Commodity prices tumbled and the United States Congress passed the controversial *Tarriff Act*. The Great Depression was no respecter of wealth or privilege, and the business interests of Fontaine Martin were now also in desperate straits. He had moved from Memphis some years earlier to found a brokerage business in New Orleans, under the name Fontaine Martin & Company. However, the firm had fallen into bankruptcy in a series of circumstances eerily similar to the cotton bale fraud perpetrated by the Martins Phillips Company in 1913. A client of the company, Mr P.J. Passera from New Orleans, had deposited substantial securities worth $90,000 ($1.5 million today) at the offices of Fontaine Martin & Company. As the business slipped into difficulties in 1929 it was alleged by Mr Passera that Fontaine Martin had illegally converted the securities into cash in a frantic attempt to keep his own company afloat. Mr Passera's lawyers had filed papers at the Biloxi Courthouse.

Also in 1929, the Canal Bank of New Orleans, Fort Worth Bank, and the Security National Bank of Wichita, sued Fontaine Martin & Company for failing to honour cheques to the value of almost $12,000 (more than $200,000 today). Fontaine Martin was, no doubt, a very concerned man, facing both bankruptcy and possible criminal proceedings.

Then an unexpected and unusual event changed everything.

The former attorney for the missing Joseph Martin, Mr S.M. Neely from Memphis, had been tasked with the administration of the final Will and Testament of the textile millionaire William Madison Wood, Joseph and Fontaine Martin's grandfather. William M. Wood - who had committed suicide in 1926 - left a fortune of $1 million (approximately $17 million today) to his eldest grandson Joseph Martin, whom he firmly believed to still be alive. The attorney Mr Neely had, in turn, been ordered to investigate and trace the missing millionaire. If Fontaine Martin could assist Mr Neely in locating his elder brother, than perhaps his own financial difficulties could be reversed. After all, he had lent Joseph $50,000 in 1913 and helped to prop up the family business at the time of his brother's strange disappearance. If he could help trace his brother's whereabouts, surely the least he could expect was to have his money returned. However, if Joseph Martin could not be traced, the money was to be widely distributed among certain charitable causes, and other members of the family, potentially leaving Fontaine with a far smaller inheritance. An urgent search for the missing millionaire was initiated – seventeen years after the previous one had ground to a halt.

William M. Wood had always maintained a strong conviction that his grandson was still alive. This belief had been reinforced in 1928 after a chance meeting with a man named Clarence S. Eldridge.

Mr Eldridge informed William M. Wood that he had been a passenger on a voyage across the Gulf of Mexico, bound for the port of Progreso, in Yucatan province, northern Mexico. During the voyage he had chatted to a fellow passenger on the steamer, who claimed to be a Mexican coffee planter called Jose Ascartin. According to Clarence Eldridge, the two men had got on well and Mr Eldridge was then invited to stay for a few nights at Ascartin's ranch in a remote village called Santa Cruz De Bravo, nestled hundreds of miles away in the state of Quintana Roo. Although the man spoke excellent Spanish, Eldridge became convinced that his host was, in fact, an American. Eventually (Eldridge claimed) the man had admitted to him that he was in fact Joseph Martin and that he had decided to disappear in 1913, *'haunted by the fear of debts.'* On his return to the United States Mr Eldridge wrote a series of letters to William M. Wood and to his solicitor Mr Neely, in which he outlined his remarkable story. The man, he claimed, was about the same age Joseph Martin would have been at that time (fifty-eight), and that he seemed strangely out in place in Mexico.

On the death of William M. Wood, as part of his duties as executor of his will, Mr Neely despatched two junior partners from his Memphis firm to make the long and arduous journey to Central America in an attempt to confirm the identity of Jose Ascartin.

The two men made the gruelling journey of more than 2,000 miles from Memphis, by steamer across the Gulf of Mexico to Progreso, then across land through Yucatan and the thickly forested Quintano Roo province, before eventually reaching the remote ranch in a settlement know as Chad, just outside Santa De Cruz Bravo.

However, the two lawyers were to be disappointed in their quest. Despite local villagers in Santa De Cruz Bravo confirming that the man calling himself Jose Ascartin had arrived in the area about the time that Joseph Martin had disappeared, those employed at Mr Ascartin's ranch remain tight-lipped. Mr Ascartin himself steadfastly denied being an American; instead claiming he had travelled to the US on business on many occasions and was therefore able to speak English well. He produced documentation in the name of Ascartin, although he would not permit his photograph to be taken. He told the two lawyers that he was 60 years of age.

Ultimately the two Americans lawyers could not positively prove that the man was Joseph Martin and were forced to leave empty handed. Conceivably, Clarence Eldridge had merely fabricated the entire tale to curry favour with the elderly and very wealthy William M. Wood. Or perhaps Mr Jose Ascartin was indeed Joseph Martin and, regretting his indiscretion in chatting so openly to Clarence Eldridge, had then made every attempt to cover his tracks.

The truth will probably never be known.

As a final footnote to the story, eight years later, in 1938, two newspapers employed a journalist and legal expert (who may possibly have been Mr S.M. Neely) to investigate the disappearance and provide a final opinion on the matter. A further visit was untaken to the remote ranch in Mexico. However, this too ended in failure, with the discovery that the man named Jose Ascartin had sold up and moved away a few months after the lawyers' visit in 1930.

Typical Farm and Plantation in Mexico

The anonymous investigator's opinion was published in 1938 under the pseudonym 'Barrister-at-Law' and is probably the closest anyone has ever been to unravelling the case of the missing millionaire:

'Even if Mr Jose Ascartin was not Mr Joseph Martin, I am quite certain that he was alive long after that April evening in 1913.

That he had £100 on him in cash was thought a likely reason for assuming robbery as a motive in his disappearance. But American visitors to London do not walk about with £100 in cash—unless they have got some ready use for it. In total, £1,100 reward was offered. Yet that did not persuade either the dark beauty or the taxi driver to come forward. For the dark beauty's non-appearance, I can account easily enough. She simply did not exist. No man in his senses tells his friends that he is going to visit an unspecified dark beauty—unless he isn't.

But the existence of the taxicab driver was concrete enough. Two respectable Londoners, Mr J. Anderson and Captain Prior, swore to his existence. A taxi driver who will not come forward is an oddity indeed - unless some person, or persons, has paid him to keep quiet.

Then there is the puzzling telegram from Vevey in Switzerland. Martin never sent it, of course. He never was at Vevey. Police enquiries established that quite clearly.

Now what would Martin have done - assuming he had wanted to disappear, and at the same time was not privy to developments in London? Send a line to a friend at Vevey asking him to send that telegram would have been one obvious course of action.

I think that Martin put £100 into his pockets that evening to very good purpose. For to tell the truth, his business was in a bad way, and it suited him very well to disappear. Liabilities against his firm were outstanding to the amount of £80,000. . .and his personal debt may have reached as high as £180,000. One bank had filed a charge against the company, of which he was president, of forging invoices for 900 bales of cotton deposited as security against a loan.

It was even said that he had raised loans on 1,800 bales where in fact only 94 existed. These matters were settled by his family (the debt of £16,000 incurred by his brother was part of the settlement). However, on the evening he disappeared, Martin did not know that his family were about to settle his debts,

With £100 in his pocket, I believe he jumped into a taxi, drove to Waterloo Station, gave the driver some earnest money to say nothing about it, and probably promised to send him some more. He then took the train to Southampton, where he boarded the Walmer Castle, bribing somebody to keep him out of the way till the boat touched at Las Palmas in the Canaries. Here he jumped the steamer before they began to look for him, and thence sent a message to Vevey to a friend to send the wire.

In a twist of events, the arrival of the telegram in London did in fact put his family somehow in touch and they conveyed money to him at Las Palmas, where he could easily have found any number of boats bound for

Central America - which is the first place of which an absconding American would think of travelling.

And there he stayed. That he should wax confidently after many years of loneliness to a fellow American whom he had met on a steamer is very natural - that he should put off that American's lawyers when they became too inquisitive is more natural still.

The only point about which I feel uncertain is the degree in which Martin's family was implicated in the affair. At first, they were quite innocent. The advertisement "Most important you should communicate with your brothers", followed by the wire from Vevey suggests that they may have known more afterwards.

Did they agree to pay off the company's debts on condition that he kept out of the way? Did they remit money to him in Mexico - and if so, why was it that they could not find him when he was named as a beneficiary in his grandfather's will in 1930? Now where there is a "will" there is generally a way for a beneficiary. Generally, but not always. My own belief is that while the Martin family kept in touch with the errant brother for some while after 1913, contact had been lost by 1930.

Perhaps they were glad to be rid of him, once they knew he was safe on a not too accessible Mexican plantation. Perhaps he was not keen to see any more of them. After all, neither he nor they could have foreseen the bequest of $1,000,000 in 1930.

Once the case was in court and the money was in dispute, I can well believe the desire to find Joseph

Martin was genuine. It is just one of those ironies that upset their best laid plans, that it was then too late.

It is just possible that Joseph Martin did not think it worth facing the consequences of certain business dealings he undertook in 1913. Even if his re-appearance in 1930 was worth $1,000,000, he preferred to remain safely obscure in Mexico. I do not think this is so, however.

It seems to me far more likely, that, cut off in his Central American retreat, he simply never heard about the will and has lived out the rest of his life without knowing of the wealth awaiting him.'

If Fontaine Martin did really know the truth about his brother's disappearance, he died in 1959 taking the secret to the grave with him.

The disappearance of Joseph Martin is still officially listed on police files as 'open and unsolved.'

Scan here for extra photographs and digital versions of the images contained in this chapter

Joseph Martin's
Grandfather –
William M. Wood

The Adventures of
Walter Drew

The History of
Quintano Roo,
Mexico

The History of the
RAC Club, Pall Mall

The Secrets of
Hungerford Bridge
(video)

"The true mystery of the world is the visible, not the invisible."
Oscar Wilde

Part One:

The southwestern corner of Vermont appears visibly peaceful and beautiful, particularly in the Fall. Vast areas of mountainous slopes hugged by a dense carpet of trees, and valleys peppered with attractive towns, lakes and rivers. Yet an area of approximately forty square miles, centred around the thickly wooded Glastenbury Mountains, is home to a series of real life puzzling missing persons mysteries; beginning in 1945 and ended in 1950.

Incorporating communities such as Bennington, Shaftsbury and Woodford, the region also includes a number of 'ghost towns'. These former communities were once part of the thriving logging and mining industry in the area, but are now abandoned, or contain just a handful of residents.

Although the Bermuda Triangle, and even the Bridgewater Triangle in south-eastern Massachusetts, may be better known, this historic part of Vermont holds a dark mystery every bit as perplexing. In fact, the area has become known as 'The Bennington Triangle', a phrase coined by the writer Joseph A. Citro. As the details unfold below, the reason for the region's mysterious name and reputation will become abundantly clear.

This story begins on Monday November 12th 1945. American soldiers had begun returning home from Europe and the Far East. The country, and the rest of the world, adjusted to the end of the war as the horrors of the concentration camps played out at the Nuremburg Trials. For many, the desire for normality was stronger than ever.

Seventy-four old Middie Rivers was an experienced hunter, outdoorsman, and mountain guide. Monday was the final day of their weekend deer hunting trip, and Middie Rivers had agreed to take a group of four hunters, including his son-in-law, on a mountain trek. Rivers, although in his seventy-fifth year, was fit and highly experienced. He also knew their intended trail well, having walked it many times before.

At 7.30am Rivers and the party set off into the hills to take full advantage of the daylight. Three hours or so passed until the group reached a fork in the trail. Rivers informed his son-in-law, Joe Lauzon, that he intended to scout the path up ahead and make sure everything was clear. As he walked off into Bickford Hollow, between Bald Mountain and Glastenbury Mountain, he told his son-in-law that he would '*only be going a short distance*' ahead, into the hollow. He took no food with him, despite Lauzon offering him some, saying that he would meet the group back at their camping spot in time for lunch. Although Bickford Hollow was also known aptly as Hells Hollow, Joe Lauzon was not concerned. He knew his father-in-law was spry; and assumed that he knew Bickford Hollow well. He last saw Rivers descending into the deep woods, in the direction of the Bickford brook.

After waiting a while, the group ate their lunch at the camping spot, Hunter's Rest near the Route 9 entrance to the Long Trail, but still Rivers did not return. Finally, when the time reached 3pm, they decided to look for their guide before darkness set in. The four men searched the trail and hillsides as best they could in the gathering gloom. Starting from the point at the fork, where Lauzon and his father-in-law had last parted company, the men searched in all directions. They fired their rifles to attract his attention and shouted out the missing man's name, but all to no avail. Eventually, as the light faded, they agreed to inform the authorities and recommence their quest in the morning.

The following morning Fire Chief Wallace Mattison together with every available firefighter began combing the area. Joe Lauzon had assumed that his father-in-law knew Bickford Hollow well, however it transpired that, although Rivers was an experienced hunter and fisherman, he did not know the dangers of the Hollow and had in fact been warned before about its dangers. Nevertheless, as he was such an experienced outdoorsman, many people were confident that he would stroll out of the woods as soon as daylight dawned.

Sadly, this was not to be the case. The team searched fruitlessly for three days and nights but could find no trace of their companion and little in the way of clues. A number of footprints were noticed on Wednesday morning; unfortunately, they could not be positively identified as River's and might have belonged to another hunter or even one of the search party, who had perhaps doubled back on themselves. By Thursday afternoon, with the men fatigued, it was decided that a bigger taskforce would be needed. An appeal for volunteers was made by Chief Mattison, who asked able-bodied searchers to report to Bradford Hooks fire station on Friday morning at 7am. Many locals joined the search parties, including other hunters and employees from River's previous place of work, the Benmont Paper Mills.

Rivers' description was issued to the *Bennington Evening Banner* in case he may have wandered elsewhere, perhaps dazed after a fall,

'Middie Rivers is about 5 feet 6 inches tall and weighs about 130 pounds. His hair is white and he wears glasses. At the time he became lost, he was wearing a red and black plaid coat, mackinaw style; brown woollen suit pants; high shoes with felt overshoes, plain gray workshirt, red and black hunting cap, gray wool sweater. He is in good health, having received a physical check-up a few months ago and was reported in fine condition.'

With the weekend approaching, a detachment of ninety-five soldiers from Fort Devens were drafted in to assist. As the large parties fanned out in several directions, beginning their systematic grid-like search, various theories began to form in the minds of the volunteers. Perhaps Rivers had suffered a heart attack and collapsed somewhere. Conceivably, he may have stumbled and fallen while crossing the brook and his body then been washed downstream by the strong currents. This notion was strengthened by the discovery a single, unspent rifle cartridge in the brook. Perhaps the cartridge had fallen from Rivers' pocket as he had tripped and been washed away by the icy waters.

However, the most popular explanation among the searchers was that the missing man had been accidently shot by another hunter who had then panicked and hidden the body. Perhaps, to avoid suspicion, the hunter had then cunningly concealed River's body in an area where it was most unlikely to be discovered, such as deep hollow, hole, or the bottom of a ravine. Conceivably, the hunter may have even joined the search himself, to avoid suspicion, and then cleverly led the quest away from the body's real location. Each man in the party looked furtively from left to right at the other searchers, secretly wondering if the guilty man stood next to them. This theory was not as far-fetched as it initially seems. On the same day as Rivers' disappearance had been reported, a man sitting in a moving railroad carriage had been accidently shoot and killed through the window, by a hunter firing at a deer from the across the fields. In addition, this theory matched another incident half a century earlier in the Bennington mountains, when a man named John Harbour had been accidently killed by a hunter's stray bullet.

However, despite men from the State Guard also joining the hunt, and a council official offering volunteers $4 a day to join the search, the quest for Middie Rivers was hindered by poor weather. Firstly, heavy rain washed away any clues and made certain areas impassable. Then, three inches of snow fell as the search entered its second week.

Eventually, it was agreed to abandon the quest and the soldiers were ordered back to Fort Devens in Massachusetts. Middie Rivers' son-in-law realised that the search to find his father-in-law alive was now probably a forlorn one, although he never gave up hope. As winter strengthened its grip, all hopes of finding the missing man's body were postponed until the spring. The only other development in the search was a belated report of a confirmed sighting, from another witness, on the day of Rivers' disappearance. Hollis Armstrong, from Safford Street in Bennington, came forward belatedly to tell investigators that he was certain that he saw a man matching Rivers' description at about 4pm on November 12th, close to the camping spot at Hunter's Rest, at which the four men had waited for their guide to return. Armstrong claimed that he warned the man to be careful in Bickford Hollow, and that the man responded that he would be fine.

As the weather finally broke at the end of March 1946 a concerted search was organised to locate the missing man. Unfortunately, available volunteers were limited and, even when numbers were bolstered by the Vermont State Guard, the area covered was not more than a few square miles. Heavy rain then fell for the majority of the five days, making conditions unpleasant and hazardous. Undeterred, nevertheless, a group of 200 men entered the woods at the junction of the Bickford and Bolles brooks in Woodford. They walked a distance of two-and-a-half miles along the left bank, into Glastenbury, before felling a tree to cross the raging torrent and then began searching the right bank. The men walked carefully, studying the ground as they moved, fanned out across the terrain. Yet, despite the intensity of the search, only one clue was forthcoming, and that came, not from the search parties, but from a lady walker, who stumbled across something while out on a Sunday hike on the mountain trails.

Mrs Eva Elwell noticed a man's handkerchief lying on the ground. It appeared to have been there for some time. Bending down to pick it up, she was surprised to discover thirty cents carefully wrapped inside. The handkerchief also displayed some dark staining. Mrs Elwell handed over the item to Chief Mattison, who immediately ordered a series of chemical tests on the marks at the Benmont Paper Mills (where Middie Rivers had once worked). It was determined that the dark stains present on the handkerchief probably corresponded with the types of inks used at the plant. At last, the search seemed to be on the right track.

However, the weather took a turn for the worse and thick snow fell in May, creating large drifts in many places, and delaying the search effort once more. The summer then meant harder ground, making tracking harder, combined with thick undergrowth which further delayed the search until the Fall.

Meanwhile, growing increasingly desperate, Middie Rivers' son-in-law Joe Lauzon announced a $100 reward to the person finding his father-in-law's body.

Regrettably, the reward yielded no further information. On the day after the discovery of the handkerchief, Joe Lauzon together with Chief Mattison paid a visit to Clara Jepson, the famous clairvoyant, who lived in Pownall on the Vermont and Massachusetts border. They did not advise her about the handkerchief. Mrs Jepson informed the searchers that she had received a strong impression of Mr Rivers stood near an old broken-down shanty. In her vision, he had walked around the shanty before making his way down a hillside. She did not think he had travelled far, however. There was a large tree nearby and, she claimed, his body would be discovered underneath it. Mrs Jepson stated that his body would be lying on its back, with one hand up to his heart, and that he had been attempting to reach some nearby water source. She also told the two men that Rivers' handkerchief would be found nearby and that it would contain money.

As Fall returned and the first anniversary of Rivers' disappearance approached, the search recommenced. Hunters in the area were warned about the dangers of accidental shootings and were advised to wear red caps. Sadly, the quest was once again fruitless. Events, however, were about to be eclipsed by yet another sinister and mysterious disappearance.

Just over a year after the loss of Middie Rivers, at 2.30pm on Sunday December 1st 1946, eighteen-year-old Bennington College sophomore student Paula Jean Welden left her residence in Dewey Hall, telling her roommate Elizabeth Johnson, *'I'm all through with studies, I'm taking a long walk.'* She was planning to go hiking along a section of the Long Trail, a 273-mile trail stretching from Massachusetts to Canada.

Paula was an attractive girl, with blue eyes, blonde hair and a fair complexion. She was fun-loving and the outdoor type, who enjoyed skating, painting, bicycling, swimming, camping, and hiking.

Paula departed wearing a lightweight red hooded parka with a fur-trimmed hood, blue jeans, and sneakers, but no heavy winter coat, despite the fact that it was already December, and the temperature was only fifty degrees Fahrenheit (ten degrees Celsius). It would drop to three degrees later in the evening, resulting in overnight snow. With sunset due in less than two hours' time, and Paula being several miles away from the entrance to the Long Trail, her reason for going out at that late hour seem an odd one. She left all her personal belongings in her dorm room (with the exception of her gold Elgin wristwatch with a black band), which seemed to indicate she had not planned on being out for long. Paula also left behind an uncashed cheque given to her by her parents.

If they intended to be out later than 11pm, Bennington College students were required to sign a logbook on leaving the premises; and to then check in with the campus security guard upon their return. There is no record of Paula doing either.

Danny Fager, the operator of the College Entrance filling station, noticed Paula walking down the driveway from the college, close to the gravel pits, then turn towards the town of Bennington.

Around 2.45pm in the afternoon, a building contractor named Louis Knapp was driving towards his home near Furnace Bridge on Route 9, just outside Bennington. He stopped to pick up a girl who was hitchhiking along College Drive, just around the corner from the college entrance. The girl matched Paula's description.

'Are you going anywhere near Route 9?' the girl enquired.

'Yes', Mr Knapp replied, *'Yes. I live a little way out, on that highway.'*

She accepted the ride, telling Mr Knapp, *'Thanks. I'm going out to the Long Trail.'*

As the girl climbed into his car, her foot slipped on the wet running board. Mr Knapp noticed her red parka and white sneakers, and politely told her to be careful. The couple chatted in the car as they headed east, and Paula appeared cheerful and untroubled.

On reaching his home, Paula got out of Mr Knapp's motorcar, said *'Thanks, that's swell'*, and walked off in the direction of the Long Trail entrance, approximately two miles to the east. When news of Paula's disappearance was reported, Mr Knapp contacted the police. He was certain about the time, as he was rushing home for his Sunday dinner, which his wife served at 3pm, and he was running a few minutes late. He also later identified the girl as Paula from a photograph and description.

Next to see Paula was Ernie Whitman, a night watchman, who was stood with three friends in Woodford Hollow at around 4pm, approximately fifty minutes after Paula had been dropped off by Louis Knapp at the Mount Glastenbury entrance to the trail. She asked Mr Whitman, *'Which way should I go to get onto the Long Trail?'*

Ernie Whitman directed her, and the group of four then watched as she crossed a bridge which led towards the trail. They all later identified the girl as Paula Welden and remembered her red, hooded parka. Another eight residents of Woodford Hollow also confirmed seeing a girl with a red parka around the same time, in the vicinity of the Fay Fuller camp, a shelter on the Long Trail.

Snow fell overnight and Paula's college roommate, Elizabeth, became increasingly worried as darkness fell and she still had not returned. When daylight dawned Elizabeth contacted college principal Lewis Webster Jones. After confirming with Paula's parents that their daughter had not returned home to Stamford, they notified Sheriff W. Clyde Peck. With the assistance of Paula's father, they immediately led a small posse to search for her. However, with three inches of fresh snow now lying on the ground, any fresh footprints left by Paula would likely be obscured. After a fruitless search, darkness fell, and it was decided to abandon the quest until the following morning. In the meantime, an appeal for Paula's whereabouts, together with a description and photograph, was issued to the *Bennington Evening Banner* and other regional papers.

However, there was to be a sensational development on Monday night, more than 130 miles away in Fall River, Massachusetts. Ora Telletier, a waitress at the Modern Restaurant in Fall River, was certain she had served a girl answering Paula's description at approximately 9.30pm (almost thirty hours after the last known sighting).

The girl had been sitting at a table with a young man, aged about twenty-five, who appeared to have been drinking. Ora told the Fall River Police that she recognised Paula from the photograph in the newspaper. She was immediately interviewed by Chief of Police McMahon, who had a wire photograph of Paula transmitted from the offices of the *Banner* to help confirm the identification. Oral Telletier informed Chief McMahon that the girl had signalled her to come over to the table while her male companion had walked over to the cashier to pay the bill. He was facing away from the table at this point.

Ora Telletier described the conversation that took place between the two women:

Paula: *'How far is it to Bennington?'*

Ora: *'Bennington, where?'*

Paula: *'Bennington, Vermont.'*

Ora: *'I don't know. You'll need to go to the bus depot.'*

Paula: *'I have to get back to Bennington. Where am I?'*

Ora: *'This is Fall Rivers.'*

Paula: *'I have to get back. I had $1,000 with me this morning, and there's none of it left!'*

With that, the young man returned and the couple left. The waitress felt vaguely uneasy about the situation and quickly connected the encounter with the report of Paula's disappearance in the newspaper. She described the young man to the police *as 'of a heavy build, about twenty-five years old, light complexion and about five feet eight inches tall. He was intoxicated and abusive.'* She added, *'the girl had not been drinking but she seemed in a dazed condition.'*

On hearing this new lead, Chief MacMahon contacted Paula's father, William Archibald Welden. He confirmed to the police that he had thought Paula may have been dating a young man (in fact, many people believed that Paula had argued with her parents over a new boyfriend, resulting in her refusing to go home for the Thanksgiving weekend). Mr Welden revealed that a young man from Stamford, who was a neighbour of the Welden's, had expressed a wish to call on Paula at the college and had been spotted hanging around the area. However, neither Chief MacMahon nor Mr

Welden knew if this unidentified young man was also missing.

Worried that Paula may have been abducted or coerced into leaving Bennington, a full police search of Fall River was organised. All hotels, boarding houses, bus, and railroad stations were searched, however no one matching Paula's description was found. A search of Fall River, with its population of over 110,000 people required a huge police effort. In addition, it would have been comparatively easy for the couple to slip away unnoticed. Nevertheless, John Proud, the manager of Adams Clothes Store in Fall River, recognised the description of the young man. Mr Proud told the police that a man closely matching the description had entered his store on the Saturday afternoon (twenty-four hours before Paula's disappearance) with two male friends and purchased a pair of boots, a red and black hat, a scarf and some hiking socks. The man had informed Mr Proud that might be going hiking and that he was a student at a photographic school in New Haven, Connecticut.

However, despite this promising lead, the man was not traced, nor did he come forward to help the police.

Another futile wide goose chase led the police to South Carolina, where a train conductor claimed to have witnessed a girl matching Paula's description boarding a westbound train.

Once again, sadly, investigators were unable to verify the sighting.

Part Two:

Rather oddly, Paula's father then took it upon himself to investigate the Falls River lead alone, without informing the authorities of his intentions. He then promptly disappeared for thirty-six hours, leading some to believe that he may have been involved in own daughter's abduction or death. Many speculated that father and daughter had disagreed over her involvement with a young man, which may have resulted in a violent argument gone tragically wrong. To make matters worse, Mr Welden could provide no proof of his daughter's alleged new boyfriend, other than a visit to a clairvoyant whom (he claimed) had told him that his daughter could be found with a man. Interestingly, the clairvoyant was the same lady, Clara Jepson, who had been consulted in the Middie Rivers case. Ultimately, however, the suspicions surrounding Paula's fathers also proved to be unfounded.

Meanwhile, back in Bennington, a further search for Paula was arranged for Wednesday 4th December. It was now approaching seventy-two hours since the last confirmed sighting of Paula. A bulldozer was then hired to excavate the gravel pit opposite the college entrance. This also proved fruitless, much to the relief of everyone involved. Next, a large group of students and lecturers from Bennington College volunteered to aid the search efforts of Sheriff Peek and there seemed to be a degree of hope when a fresh set of tracks in the snow was located by one of college lecturers. The footprints were located on the Bald Mountain trail leading back to the outskirts of Bennington, and appeared to have been made by a small pair of sneakers.

However, while this gave everyone involved some hope that Paula might still be at large, the trail did not lead the team any closer to finding Paula, either dead or alive.

The search grid was widened around the hill covered slopes of the Glastenbury Mountain, based on the assumption that the missing girl may have wandered away from the Long Trail. However, temperatures dropped significantly on Friday 6th, and it was decided to abandon ground efforts on the mountain sides, as snow drifted and ice formed.

In another strange coincidence, William Lauzon (the son of Joe Lauzon, the man who had reported Middie Rivers missing a year earlier from Hunter's Rest campsite) notified the authorities that on the day of Paula's disappearance, three army servicemen had passed through Hunters' Rest. The three men did not seem appropriately attired for hiking on the Long Trail, particularly in winter. They were also carrying a suitcase. William Lauzon, who managed Hunters' Rest campsite, agreed to store the suitcase for the men while they walked on. They never returned to collect it. As part of their investigation into Paula's disappearance, the authorities in Bennington decided to open the suitcase. It contained documents which identified the three men as William Watts, J.W. Carrol, and M. Golder. The case remained unclaimed.

In the meantime, an elderly couple, Mr & Mrs Rice, came forward claiming that they had seen a girl in a red parka, walking on the Long Trail, on the day of Paula's disappearance. The girl was only 100 yards ahead of the elderly couple when she turned a corner on the pathway, and they lost sight of her for a moment behind the thick trees. However, when they reached the corner, the girl had completely vanished. They looked in all directions, but were unable to see her.

Despite the evidence of the waitress from the Modern Restaurant in Fall River, and a cab driver named Abe Ruskin who claimed to have dropped off a young girl in a red coat at Bennington Bus station around 8.30pm on Sunday evening, State's Attorney Jerome firmly believed that Paula would still be found in the mountain area around Bennington and decided to continue the search efforts there. The following morning, a sweep of a seven square mile area between Glastenbury and Bald Mountains was made by five aircraft from the local airfield at Bennington. Local pilots, Gary Buckley, Bob Saursville, and Bill Freitag placed themselves at the disposal of the search teams, together with two more planes belonging to a friend of Paula's family from Stamford, Mr Tuck.

With one week now having passed since Paula's disappearance the effort was renewed. 120 men were drafted in from the Bennington district State Guard, together with another tranche of local volunteers, all fully prepared to brave the icy conditions. Large amounts of confetti were purchased, and each volunteer was told to sprinkle confetti behind them as they searched, to ensure the same areas were not covered twice. The intensive combing of the area continued for several more days, both by land and air, but without any positive result. Paula's case received a substantial amount of press coverage (far more the disappearance of Middie Rivers) and officials from other states and agencies were drafted in by Governor Ernest Gibson to assist in the ongoing investigation. These included Police Commissioner Edward J. Hickey, Lieutenant Robert Rundle from the Connecticut State Police, and State Investigator Almo Franzoni. Paula's father, together with Franzoni, and with the cooperation of the F.B.I., raised a reward of $5,000 for the recovery of a, still alive, Paula. This amount offered (reducing to $2,000 for the recovery of her body) equates to more than $75,000 today and was a substantial inducement.

However, despite the investigators' endeavours, little progress was made. Eventually the search was wound down. Bennington residents looked uneasily over their shoulders as rumours began to circulate that foul play was the most probable cause of Paula's death. Stories that Paula had argued with her family over not returning home for Thanksgiving persisted. Many journalists also reported that William Welden was dissatisfied with the efficiency of the search effort. Conceivably as a result of this, or perhaps due to direct pressure from Paula's father in Stamford, noted private detective Raymond C. Schindler was discreetly retained by the *Stamford Advocate* newspaper to investigate the case. No announcement was made of Schindler's involvement until he had been given the opportunity to review the evidence and interview the crucial witnesses.

Schindler approached the case from the different viewpoint and asked one important question. Why, despite the efforts of 500 searchers and five aircraft, had no one managed to locate the missing girl's body? This led Schindler to ask himself three further questions:

What if Louis Knapp (the witness who picked up Paula) had been mistaken?

What if the other witnesses had mistaken someone else for Paula, that afternoon?

And, what if Paula never actually reached the Long Trail?

Mindful of this, Schindler adopted the presumption that the answer to these three questions was 'yes' and set about re-interviewing the witnesses.

Firstly, he concluded, the search effort had been genuinely thorough and exhaustive. If Paula had died on the mountain that night, it was almost certain her body would have been located. But, if she never in fact reached the Long Trail, then it seemed probable that she had either disappeared voluntarily or been abducted, before ever reaching the mountain path. Based on this assumption, he visited Louis Knapp at his home.

Mr Knapp repeated the story he had told the police, confirming that he was certain the girl who hailed a ride outside Bennington College that day was Paula Welden. This time, however, his story differed slightly from that originally reported. Mr Knapp stated that the coat worn by the girl that day was brown and not red.

Paula's friends at college and her father had all previously confirmed that her parka was red in colour. As a test, Mr Knapp was asked to name the colour of two red objects in the room and the colour of a maroon scarf that the interviewer was wearing. To all three he replied '*brown.*' Furthers tests then revealed that the main witness in the search for Paula Welden was, in fact, colour blind.

Furthermore, in this version of the events, Mr Knapp told the private detective that the girl had been '*noticeably quiet and talked very little*' during the short journey. This appears to be at odds to the report given my Mr Knapp at his earlier interview, in which he described her as cheerful and chatty. Conceivably, Mr Knapp (not wishing to appear at odds with newspaper speculation regarding the missing girl), had revised his opinion on Paula's mood. Certainly, the weight of evidence from other witnesses, such as Elizabeth Johnson, seemed to be that Paula was '*despondent*' in the days prior to her disappearance.

Mr Knapp continued his statement, adding '*We reached the house around 3.10pm, the girl thanked me and walked off in the direction of the Long Trail entrance*', which was two miles further east along Route 9.

Immediately on entering his house Louis Knapp went to wash his hands, ready for dinner. While the family waited to eat, his young daughter ran outside to play in the front yard. A maximum of only four minutes passed, before Mrs Knapp went into the yard to tell their daughter that dinner was ready. Neither of them noticed anybody walking down the road, in either direction. Raymond Schindler observed that from the Knapp property the road extended, in a straight line, for at least a clear half mile towards the Long Trail intersection. It would have been impossible for Paula to have passed out of sight so quickly, if she had indeed been walking towards the Long Trail entrance. Neither Mr and Mrs Knapp, or his daughter, noticed a single car on the road (of this, they were certain), however it was possible that a motorist may have picked up Paula in the few moments between Mr Knapp heading indoors and his daughter going outside to play. If so, had it been a prearranged meeting, or a chance encounter? A chance encounter seemed the more probable, since Paula could not have known that she would have been on that exact stretch of highway at that precise moment.

To further strengthen Schindler's theory of foul play, no driver came forward to admit picking up a girl on Route 9 on December 1st, despite the appeal for witnesses being widespread. If a car did stop and pick up Paula on that lonely stretch of road on that Sunday afternoon, then the driver clearly had something to hide.

Credibility was added to this potential twist in the tale by another witness who came forward, claiming to have spotted a maroon-coloured car, containing a young man and two young women, leaving Bennington later that day. However, this vehicle was never traced.

Next, Raymond Schindler pondered the evidence of the elderly couple who had witnessed a girl in a red coat 100 yards ahead of them on the Long Trail. Had they been mistaken? After all, the girl had her back to the couple and disappeared from sight quickly afterwards. This theory gathered further momentum when Schindler and his team discovered that the road sign at the Long Trail intersection, pointing in the direction of the path, had actually been knocked down in the days before Paula's disappearance and was lying in the undergrowth, not visible to a passer-by, especially to someone such as Paula, who had never visited the Trail before and was unfamiliar with that stretch of road. Yet, sixty yards beyond the main Long Trail intersection on Route 9 was another sign saying 'Long Trail', which pointed along a different path leading towards Sucker Pond, and which snaked continuously away from the main Long Trail path. It would have been an easy mistake for Paula to have made in the fading light, especially being unfamiliar with the area. Furthermore, although the actual Long Trail had been searched thoroughly, this second path had not been. Had the authorities been searching in the wrong place?

Whatever assumptions Raymond Schindler and the other investigators made, the heavy winter snowfall meant that all search efforts would now need to be delayed until the spring thaw of 1947.

Renewed efforts were made to find some trace of Paula during the early summer of 1947, but, alas, not a single clue would ever be found. She seemed to have simply vanished from the earth. For several years, on the anniversary of her disappearance, Paula's family, along with several newspapers, published a timely reminder, together with a renewed appeal for information.

However, it would be many years before any new leads appeared in the hunt for Paula Welden. In the meantime, once again, another mysterious occurrence would rock the town of Bennington – exactly three years to the day after Paula Welden vanished. This time it would be even more bizarre and inexplicable.

James Edward Tedford was a Great War veteran who had previously lived near Franklin in Vermont. Although in his sixties, he had been happily married for several years to a much younger woman, twenty-eight-year-old Pearl. However, in 1946 events took an unexpected turn. James Tedford returned home one day to find the house empty. Pearl was supposed to be at home but was nowhere to be seen. The house appeared completely normal, there was no sign of a disturbance, in fact there was even signs that Pearl had been preparing a meal for his return.

Not unduly concerned, James Tedford merely assumed that she had stepped out for a moment. When evening, and then night, came, and then passed, and Pearl had still not returned, Tedford began to worry. Enquiries were made, and several witnesses reported seeing Pearl walking towards the Amoco store in town, apparently in good spirits.

According to local speculation at that time, no trace nor clue of Pearl Tedford was ever found. Many sources have erroneously reported that she was never seen again.

The sudden disappearance of his wife saw James Tedford fall into a deep depression.

He became a virtual recluse who barely left his house. Eventually, in 1947, Tedford moved into the Soldier's Retirement Home in Bennington – not far from the college campus where Paula Weldon had vanished. Here he lived a quiet and solitary life. He only occasionally left the retirement home, to visit relatives who lived in St. Albans, Vermont - an eight-hour bus ride north on Route 7 through the Green Mountain wilderness area.

At Thanksgiving in 1949 (now aged sixty-five) he again decided to visit his relatives in St Albans. Tedford informed the staff at the rest home that he would be travelling back to Bennington on December 1st - the third anniversary of Paula's disappearance. He boarded the bus in St Albans, along with at least fifteen other passengers, stowed his luggage, appearing to be his typically dour and sullen self. Several passengers noticed him asleep during the journey, with an open bus timetable on the seat next to him.

However, Tedford did not arrive back at his Bennington retirement home as scheduled. Both the bus driver and the fifteen passengers testified that they had seen James Tedford board the bus in St Albans. This fact was confirmed by the discovery of his luggage, cash, and all his belongings, which were found still located in the luggage rack on the bus. Even the open bus timetable remained on the empty seat next to the one occupied by Tedford. According to his fellow passengers, they had all seen him board, many had seen him sleeping soundly in his seat, yet no one had witnessed him leave the bus. In fact, it was not until the bus reached its ultimate destination, that anyone noticed that he was gone. Tedford simply vanished into thin air – as his wife had done, and just like Paula Welden did three years earlier. It has been claimed that the bus made no stops en route, and that James Tedford simply disappeared into the ether. This seems farfetched. However, the area was already developing a reputation for unusual activity. For at least 100 years prior to 1949 there had been numerous sightings of a 'Bigfoot'-like creature in the mountains, known as the 'Bennington Monster'. In addition, the area had become well known for strange and unexplained UFO sightings. Many locals simply assumed that Tedford had been abducted by some strange force, which accounted for his complete disappearance. The area is also steeped in ancient Native American folklore. The Abenaki tribe, who buried their dead at its base, believed that the Glastenbury Mountain was cursed. The strange vortex of wind patterns surrounding the mountain, onto which the wind appeared to blow from all four directions at once, was also believed to account for many of the strange occurrences in the area.

But what really happened to James Tedford. Did he actually vanish from the bus unnoticed? Did he commit suicide, or had he been abducted during a comfort break at one of the scheduled bus stops along Route 9? But, if so, why did he leave all his luggage and cash on board? And why did so many potential witnesses fail to see him leave the bus?

Leaving aside the mystical, the paranormal, and the sensational reporting of this story on certain websites, some further research does reveal more information, and even one possible solution.

Most importantly, Reginald Buzzell, the manager of the soldiers' retirement home, James did not actually report James Tedford missing on the day of his disappearance. Although it was assumed that Tedford would be returning on December 1st, his failure to do so was not notified to the authorities until December 7th. At this juncture the Public Safety Department at Montpelier issued a twelve-state alarm, together with a description of Tedford:

'A veteran of World War 1. Tedford weighs 116 pounds is five feet five inches tall and is slightly hunched. He was wearing a gray suit and army overcoat when he disappeared on Dec 1st.'

All bus terminals on the route from St Albans to Bennington were checked on December 7th and 8th by State police officers. It was initially reported that no one could remember seeing James Tedford alighting the bus. However, a police officer in Brattleboro stated that he noticed a man exactly matching Tedford's description alighting a bus at Brattleboro station between 3pm and 4pm on December 1st. He was confident that the man was Tedford. Unfortunately, as a week had now passed since the disappearance, officials were unable to trace the mystery man.

In addition to searching bus stations along Route 9, State police also checked in Cambridge, Vermont, in the hope that Tedford had returned to his original hometown. However, this potential lead also drew a blank.

James Tedford's relatives in St Albans confirmed that they had accompanied him to the bus station on December 1st, and could confirm that he was definitely aboard the southbound bus when it departed the station. Over the coming days, two more potential witnesses also came forward. State police officers in Rutland were contacted by a bus driver who thought he may have seen Tedford getting of a bus at Brandon at 8pm on the night of December 1st. However, the sighting was unconfirmed, since the description given by the driver differed slightly from the one given by Tedford's family. Nevertheless, the driver was certain that the man was James Tedford. Further credibility was added to this possible sighting when Brandon Police Chief Edward Phelps was contacted by a local cab driver, James Tierney, who reported seeing a man exactly matching Tedford's description around 11pm on December 1st. The man was wearing an army overcoat, a beret style hat, light trousers, and appeared to be acting strangely. A search was made for the man, but he was never traced.

The next lead came on December 13th, when a previous acquaintance of Tedford's came forward, claiming to have seen the missing man hitch-hiking near Vergennes, roughly twenty-seven miles from Brandon. Again, a search was made for the man, but again the lead proved to be a fruitless one.

There is one possible solution to the mystery, however. It was not generally reported at the time, but it was believed that James Tedford may have recently discovered the whereabouts of his young wife. An obscure detail, noted in a long-forgotten police file, mentions some interviews that were conducted with several St Albans' residents following Tedford's disappearance. It is possible that he had discovered Pearl was now living close to St Albans, in Burlington, on the shores of Lake Champlain, and that he planned to visit her while in the area. Police records also show that Tedford only purchased a single bus ticket from Bennington to St Albans, rather than his usual return fare. It is conceivable that he never intended to return to the Soldiers' rest home in Bennington at all. Perhaps, instead, his intention was to seek a reconciliation with Pearl, and when this failed, he left distraught and suffered a relapse of his depression. Later enquiries discovered that, when the time came to leave St Albans on the morning of December 1st, his family took him directly to the bus station. Once there, he purchased a single ticket – not to Bennington - but only as far as Burlington. He then boarded the bus, probably without his family realising he had not purchased a ticket back to Bennington. At Burlington, police interviews with the driver on the Vermont Transit Co. line confirmed that Tedford left the bus there for a few hours (perhaps to attempt a reconciliation with Pearl before then reboarding a later southbound bus to Bennington). Based on the possible sightings of Tedford in and around Brandon, it is most likely that he alighted there unnoticed, among the coming and going of other passengers, and vanished into the darkness of a winter's night. Also, in his state of upset and confusion, leaving his possessions still aboard the bus. Remember, he left an open bus timetable on the seat next to him. Why do this unless you intended to leave the bus at a different stop to his usual, often-made journey to Bennington? Once alone, he then wandered, depressed and suicidal, until he succumbed to the weather, took his own life, or met another dark and unknown fate.

No further evidence or clues were ever found and the disappearance of James Tedford remains – like those of Middie Rivers and Paula Welden – another Bennington enigma.

Meanwhile, time passed, with little in the way of encouragement for the families of Middie Rivers, Paula Welden, and James Tedford. The Vermont State Police was formed in 1947, partially as a result of William Welden's open criticism of the local police response to his daughter's disappearance. State's investigator Almo Franzoni arrested and questioned John Bush, a thirty-two-year-old man from West Rutland who had been seen flashing a roll of dollar bills on December 1st 1946, and telling friends about *'having a date with a blonde in Bennington on Sunday afternoon'*. He was already known to the police over a string of car thefts and Franzoni wondered if the maroon car seen on the day of Paula's disappearance may have contained John Bush and Paula Welden. However, Bush denied ever knowing or meeting Paula and this line of investigation ultimately stalled.

The attention of Bennington's residents, along with the eyes of the media, was diverted by the growing Cold War between the US and Russia, as 1950 turned from spring into summer. Albert Einstein warned of the threat of world destruction, while President Truman ordered the development of the hydrogen bomb in response to the Soviet Union's recent detonation of their first atomic bomb.

However, in the Fall, the spotlight once again returned to the series of mysterious missing persons cases in and around the Bennington area. Yet another inexplicable occurrence was to take place on Thursday October 12th 1950.

Part Three:

An eight-year-old boy named Paul Jepson was last seen playing in his family's pickup truck. Paul's mother had left her son waiting in the truck while she tended to some pigs at the Bennington dump site, at which she and her husband were caretakers. The five-acre site was completely fenced in and contained within a larger fifty-acre wooded area. Paul's mother left her son out of sight *'for a few minutes'* while she fed the pigs. She had done so on many occasions before and the dump site was empty at the time. When she returned, Paul had vanished without a trace.

Bennington County Sheriff John H. Maloney organised a party of deputies, game wardens and volunteer firefighters, who searched the area diligently until darkness set in. Floodlights were then utilised, as were patrols on nearby roads and a door-to-door search at the twenty-five properties nearest the site. No trace of Paul could be found.

The following day Sheriff Maloney contacted Sheriff Arthur N. Jennison from Keene, New Hampshire, who arrived with a pair of specially trained bloodhounds. The dogs were given the boy's scent and set up in pursuit. There is no doubt that the hounds managed to pick up Paul Jepson's trail, however the scent ended abruptly by the Long Trail intersection on the Route 9 Highway, just outside Bennington. This suggested to the investigating team that Paul may have been picked up by a passing car. In an even more sinister development, the spot at which the boy's scent suddenly vanished was the exact spot at which Paula Welden had last been seen four years earlier.

Despite the fact that Paul was wearing a red coat, which should have made him easy to spot, no sightings or clues were forthcoming. Matters were made more difficult by unhelpful local rumours that the boy's parents had killed him and feed him to the pigs. When this was disproved, superstition and folklore fuelled speculation even more. Had Paul been attacked by the Bennington Monster or abducted by aliens? The police ignored such rumours and continued their quest to recover the boy. Paul's father told the *Albany Times Union* newspaper that his son had been fascinated by the thought of exploring '*the lure of the mountains*', and may have just wandered off. Seemingly, his son had *'talked of nothing else for days'* before he disappeared.

If Paul had become lost and disoriented in the few crucial hours following his disappearance, police resources utilised in finding him were critically hampered in that all-important period. Firstly, a motorist in North Hoosick, New York State, saw a boy resembling Paul's description wandering on the road in the direction of the Vermont State line. Her description of the boy was similar, which initiated another quest for Paul many miles from the original site, however this rapidly became another frustrating red herring, when the boy could not be located.

Police resources were then further strained when another Bennington boy went missing just one week later. A description and photograph were issued for eleven-year-old Larry Benyon who had vanished after an argument with his parents and school, over his use of an air rifle. Following another huge search effort, the boy promptly walked out of the forest the following morning, having made his own campfire and survived the night on a bag of apples and doughnuts he had taken with him!

Meanwhile, more false hope in the search for Paul Jepson came with reports of a boy seen hiding in an old quarry in Manchester, however, once again, this proved to be yet another false trail.

With Paul's mother distraught and under sedation, State's Attorney Waldo Holden called a huge conference of all agencies involved in the hunt for the missing boy. Another huge effort was made, extending into the Bald Mountain area and involving many volunteers from local factories and from Bennington College. Eventually, however, as the weather worsened, the authorities were forced to scale down the search effort. Not a single clue or shred of evidence was ever found despite the huge endeavours of everyone involved. However, once again, yet another event was about to grip the town of Bennington with fear.

Just sixteen days after Paul Jepson had vanished, another strange disappearance rocked the community. Experienced walker and outdoors woman, fifty-three-year-old Frieda Langer, left her home in North Adams at 12.15pm on Saturday October 28th. Together with her husband, Max Langer, and cousin, Herbert Elsner, the trio planned to journey to a camping site near Somerset Pond. The trio had visited the same site virtually every weekend for the past decade. After arriving at the camp site, Herbert Elsner and Frieda Langer headed out to see if they could stir up some pheasants to hunt. Mr Langer, who no longer had a hunting license due to his poor eyesight, remained at the camp. Mrs Langer and Mr Elsner walked around the bend in the shoreline, climbed the low ridge behind the camp and made their way approximately 150 yards down the wooded ravine on the far side, until they reached Harrison Brook, one of the many streams that feed into the Somerset Pond. Mr Elsner jumped across the brook; however, Mrs Langer slipped and tumbled on the wet stones falling into the water. It was only a minor mishap, and the pair laughed it off. Unfortunately, Mrs Langer's brown whipcord trousers were now soaking wet, so she decided to return to their campsite and change them. Mr Elsner offered to accompany her, but she declined, telling him it was only a few yards over the ridge. She walked off, out of sight, while her cousin waited for her return.

Elsner lingered for fifteen minutes or so. When Frieda did not return, he concluded that she had decided to stay at the camp after all. He continued hunting for a short while before returning to the camp at 4.45pm. It was still daylight. Max Langer looked surprised to see him,

'Where's Frieda?', he said.

'Isn't she here, Max? Didn't she come back to the camp?'

When the two men realised that Frieda hadn't returned they decided to quickly search for her, before darkness fell. Neither man was immediately worried as Mr Langer later explained,

'She knows this country like a book, because she's trampled all over here every weekend for the past ten years. She's a better hunter than most men.'

After their initial search proved negative, they walked to the nearby Somerset Dam, where the caretaker there contacted the State police at Brattleboro. Within one hour a vanguard of troopers and volunteers arrived and conducted an all-night search in the area. Under Deputy Sheriff Roy Hood, troopers from Brattleboro, Bennington, Burlington, Rutland, Middlebury, Bellow Falls, and St Albans joined the effort. Bonfires were lit along the shore road and flashlights issued to every man. Mr Langer explained to the police that he had never left the camp, so Mrs Langer could not have come back to change her clothes without him noticing. A brief glance at the Langer's campsite confirmed this. There were no wet clothes or indications that she had returned.

At dawn the following day more volunteers reinforced the search teams, and a 5,000-acre site was meticulously combed. Groups of thirty men fanned out from the campsite and combed every square inch of ground. Later in the day a reliable bloodhound was brought to the scene by Deputy Sheriff Trembley. The dog was given Frieda Langer's scent from another item of clothing and immediately picked up her trail. Beginning at the brook, where Mr Elsner had last seen her, the dog followed the scent straight back to the campsite. The test was repeated seven times, and the bloodhound always returned to the campsite. Not once did the animal detect the scent heading in any other direction. This was reinforced by the fact that no footprints were found on the soft ground near the water's edge.

The search teams were bamboozled. Frieda Langer appeared to have either returned to the campsite – or vanished into thin air.

Max Langer offered a possible solution to the police. According to her husband, Frieda Langer had undergone surgery for a brain tumour five years previously and as a result had occasionally suffered from blackouts and dizzy spells. He thought it was possible that her tumble into the icy water of the brook may have induced another seizure.

However, she had not suffered any such incident for at least eighteen months; and this still did not account for the bloodhound's failure to detect her scent heading in any other direction apart from straight back to their campsite.

A description was issued, in case Frieda Langer had wandered further afield, although there were very few houses in the vicinity and only a dirt road leading to the Molly Stark trail about a quarter of a mile from the campsite,

'Mrs Freida Langer was last seen wearing a red woollen shirt under a brown suede jacket, with brown

whipcord trousers and knee-high hunting pack shoes. Her dark, slightly curly hair was uncovered.'

An air search involving a combination of small planes, a helicopter, and a seaplane, scoured the hillsides and the lake, to no avail. The shore section of the lake was patrolled by boat, although the water levels were low, making it unlikely anybody could have accidentally drowned.

The strange circumstances surrounding Mrs Langer's disappearance perplexed the authorities. They decided to investigate further. A complete stranger to the area was employed to retrace the walk from Harrison's Brook, back to the Langer's camp. It transpired that even someone with no previous knowledge the region or the landscape found it almost impossible to get lost. Heading towards the camp, the lake was clearly visible through the trees, as were the roofs of other camps. Steep, mountainous slopes loomed behind the terrain on one side, making it easy for even a novice to realise if they had turned in the wrong direction. The area was wooded, but not densely, and at the time Frieda Langer was supposed to be retracing her steps to the camp, the sun would have been setting directly behind the camp and pond, acting like a giant marker.

Perhaps under the instructions of State's investigator Almo Franzoni (who, it had been rumoured, was drafted in to assist in this increasingly more baffling case), the police began questioning the Langer's neighbours in North Adam. In the meantime, Max Langer remained at the campsite refusing to return home until his wife was found. He even offered a reward of $100 for information leading to his wife's recovery.

All those who knew the Langers and Herbert Elsner confirmed that they were friendly and devoted, in fact, no one could remember them ever arguing. However, a chance remark by Max Langer puzzled the police. Despite originally telling investigators that he had remained at the camp during the whole time his wife and Herbert Elsner had been away, he mentioned to others later that he had left for a short time. He was forced to clarify his earlier statement by saying that he had *'always remained within the vicinity of the camp.'* Nevertheless, the police decided to subject both men to a lie detector test, and they were taken to Rhode Island (both men agreed voluntarily to the tests). The results of the first test proved inclusive, and a second test was ordered. This also proved inclusive. These unsatisfactory results failed to help the police in anyway, since they neither confirmed nor denied any suspicions they might have harboured and merely took resources away from the quest to discover Mrs Langer's whereabouts.

After a week, search efforts were suspended. The wet weather had worsened, wiping away most ground evidence, and the State troopers were drafted elsewhere to help search for another lost boy in Burlington.

Despite a nationwide appeal in the hunt for Freida Langer, fresh leads were few and far between. A streetcar operator in Boston thought he had spotted a woman matching Freida Langer's description riding the city's streetcar. However, this lead proved unfounded. Detectives examined every address in Mrs Langer's notebook, but she was not to be found at any of those homes. When a witness spotted a couple burning, what appeared to be, a woman's clothing on the side of the highway in West Wardsboro, police raced to the scene. However, this also proved to be unrelated to the case.

Eventually, although Max Langer never gave up hope of finding his wife, the search effort was wound down. No more clues were forthcoming until one day, more than six months later.

Two Stamford fishermen, James Renton and Herman Lincoln, discovered Frieda Langer's badly decomposed body three miles away from the campsite, on the east bank of the Deerfield River. In the series of five strange disappearances described in this chapter, Frieda's was the only case in which the victim's body was actually found.

The grisly discovery was made by the two fishermen on May 12th 1951, approximately three miles from the ravine where Freida Langer had last been seen alive. Her badly deteriorated corpse was found lying close at the foot of a steep bank, close to a deep, water-filled hole, which was cloaked with long grass and thick undergrowth. So badly decomposed and water damaged was the body that an identification was only possible due to the metal plate located in Freida Langer's skull (from her brain surgery some years earlier). It was also extremely difficult to determine an exact cause of death, although Dr Milton Wolfe was able to ascertain that her skull was intact and that no bones had been broken. Nevertheless, a verdict of 'accidental drowning' was recorded. It was surmised that Mrs Langer has wandered, perhaps in a daze following a seizure, and fallen into the deep chasm.

There was a moment of drama when the State's Attorney delayed Mrs Langer's burial to order a further medical opinion on the cause of death, however the second examination agreed with the first, and a verdict of accidental death remained the most likely reason for Freida Langer's demise. She was buried at Southview Cemetery in North Adam on May 15th. Max Langer was heartbroken. He had remained hopeful, against all odds, that his wife would be found alive somewhere. Nevertheless, he paid the promised $100 reward to James Renton and Herman Lincoln.

The two most baffling aspects of Freida Langer's disappearance have often been questioned. Firstly, why was her body found over three miles from the place in which she was last seen? And, secondly, the fact that her body was discovered in an area that had been searched many times during the original investigation, yet, nobody had seen it. Why? Had she been killed somewhere else, and her body then dumped by the Deerfield River?

Again, many sensationalist websites have speculated widely as to the reason. However, the official and most plausible explanation, given by State's Attorney Edward John and Dr Milton Wolfe, was that Freida Langer had wandered in the dark, dazed and perhaps mentally incapacitated, before eventually falling down the deep hole (next to which her body was found). During the original search effort, the hole had been hidden by undergrowth, stopping the search teams from even realising it was there. Then, during the spring high waters, when the brooks and underground sources had become swollen with melted snow, her body floated to the surface and was deposited on the ground beside the hole.

And, so, there appeared to be a plausible answer to the riddle surrounding the death of Freida Langer. Yet, as the years marched on, there was to be no such closure for the families of Middie Rivers, Paula Welden, James Tedford, and Paul Jepson.

Every few years the newspapers would refresh the appeal for information, in the hope that someone would come forward. In March 1953, a bizarre discovery in Bennington triggered hope of a resolution. A discarded, homemade, wooden box was uncovered in a Pownal dump (close to the last known whereabouts of Paul Jepson), which contained a number of human bones. The news of the discovery immediately fuelled hope that the bones might by those of Paula Welden and Paul Jepson. However, an examination by State Pathologist Dr Joseph Spelman concluded that the bones were merely scientific exhibits that had been used by medical students at Bennington College.

Many continued to believe that Paula Welden planned her own disappearance. Others thought she was abducted and killed by a hunter. Yet from that day to this, there has been no confirmed sighting of the missing girl. There was a brief moment of hope in September of 1952, when a Readsboro man, Fred Gaudette, claimed that he could *'locate Paula Welden's body within a few yards.'* Gaudette was arrested and police officers were about to undertake a dig for Paula's remains, when he admitted that he made the whole thing up as a joke to impress friends.

1958 brought suspicions of a bizarre serial killer targeting victims with the same initials, when Polly Whitman, another eighteen-year-old college student with the same initials as Paula Welden went missing. This also proved to be another false dawn.

Excluding the discovery of Freida Langer's body, the police are no closer now to solving the disappearances than they were more than seventy years ago. Yet the five mysterious cases discussed in this story are not the end of the tale. There have been many other equally baffling missing persons cases in Vermont, fuelling speculation ranging from UFO abduction to a prolific serial killer operating in the state.

Carl Herrick vanished in November 1943. However, as his body was eventually found, this incident is frequently overlooked in discussions about the series of disappearances in the Bennington area.

Herrick had been hunting with his cousin Henry in an area to the northeast of Glastenbury Mountain. When the pair became separated, Henry contacted authorities. After a few days, searchers located Herrick's body. Lying next to his body was his rifle, however no bullets had been discharged. The post-mortem determined that the cause of death was *'Squeezing: The victim's ribs having punctured his lungs'*.

There have been as many as forty people reported missing in the area, all in equally unusual circumstances, including the cases of Francis Christman and Martha Jeanette Jones in the 1950s. Some have been resolved, others remain an enigma. The ancient and cursed reputation of the mountains, together with the large number of alleged Bigfoot and UFO sighting in the Bennington area have both been used as an explanation for the strange disappearances. Others have suggested that a wild animal, such as a bobcat, mountain lion, lynx, or even the (thought to be extinct) catamount may have been responsible. This seems unlikely, however, as these animals are not known to be aggressive towards humans and usually prefer to avoid contact. In addition, no torn clothing, blood, or remains were ever discovered to indicate such an explanation.

A more interesting possibility is the serial killer theory. Remember, in the 1940s and '50s, the term 'serial killer' had yet to be coined. Although 'continuing killers' or 'repeat killers' were not unheard of, the psychology of this type of murderer was not yet fully understood and, as a consequence, less likely to have been considered at the time. Whilst it is highly unlikely that a serial killer may have been responsible for all the disappearances in the Bennington region, it is certainly feasible that such a killer may be accountable for, at least, some of the unsolved vanishings.

Investigators tend to look for similarities and characteristics to mark the work of a serial murderer. There are certainly some in the strange catalogue of events described in this story. All of those missing were last seen alive between 3pm – 4pm and in the same general geographical area. All the disappearances occurred in a five-year period and all at the same time of year, between the beginning of October and December 1st, with two taking place on the same day. The victims were always alone at the time of the disappearance in locations which were not overlooked, meaning that the presence of witnesses was an unlikely one. Does this suggest someone who knew the area, or whose work patterns enabled them to pass through the region unquestioned during the final three months of the year? The possibility of a hunter or businessman who travelled freely, and without suspicion, to the Bennington area between October and December each year is a distinct possibilty. With the exception of Freida Langer, no trace of the victims or their clothes were ever found. Neither was a crime scene located, perhaps meaning that a potential killer had a vehicle nearby. This makes the probability of a highly skilled and experienced serial killer more probable than, say, an attack by a mountain lion or a lynx. However, because of the varied age, type, and gender variation of the victims, it is unlikely that a serial killer can be blamed for all of the disappearances. As the years pass, one thing seems certain - that the Bennington mystery merely seems to deepen. Yet, the only truth on which we can firmly rely, is that we will probably never know what really happened to Middie Rivers, Paula Welden, Paul Jepson, James Tedford and Freida Langer.

Scan here for extra photographs and digital versions of the images contained in this chapter

Article on James
Tedford

Bennington Triangle
Documentary

Detective Raymond
Schindler

Guide to The Long Trail

How Many More
Went Missing

Paula Weldon Mini
Documentary

The Bennington
Myths

The Empty House

"Husband? I never found a man good enough for that."
Marlene Dietrich, *Morocco* (1930)

Part One:

The painting 'Boulevard of Broken Dreams', by Gottfried Heinwein, reveals a darker side of the Tinseltown dream. Even during the 1930s and '40s, the so-called golden era of the movies, the streets of Hollywood were not always paved with gold. For every aspiring starlet dreaming of a plaque on the Hollywood Walk of Fame, or glamorous millionaire drawn downtown by the bright neon lights, there were a multitude of meaner streets, littered with numerous tragic tales. Hundreds of cast aside actors eking out a living, haunted by broken promises, missed opportunities, and out-of-reach dreams of what might have been. Even away from the sparkle of the silver screen, fortunes were lost as well as made, often through gambling, drinking, or simply, ostentatious overspending. In chapters four and five of *Erased,* we explore two such stories, both remarkably similar. Similar enough, in fact, to reopen one of Hollywood's ugliest wounds. Both victims (if, indeed, they were victims at all) suddenly vanished without a trace; only six weeks apart and just a few miles from each other. The solution to both cases baffled the L.A. police and the victim's families alike, each one seemingly lifted from the pages of the latest Raymond Chander novel.

In the years that followed the war, the showbusiness sparkle of the silver screen masked the malevolent side of Los Angeles. Rumours of gangland hits, and buried bodies beneath the lush orange groves, tainted the tinsel of Hollywood. For, beneath the glamour of 1940s Los Angeles, lurked the spectre of crime. Organised criminal mobsters and an unsolved spate of murders involving attractive young women haunted the City of Angels; handicapped as it was by a police department tainted by corruption. It is perhaps not surprising, then, that the movie studios of Hollywood responded with a string of dark, stylised, and complex crime thrillers which would become known as the genre of *film noir*. These movies, with titles such as *The Maltese Falcon, Out of the Past, Crossfire,* and *Dead on Arrival* – each filled with murder, mystery and menace - packed the movie theatres of America, every one seemingly darker, and more complex, than the last.

However, a series of real-life dramas competed for with the movies for dramatic headlines during the late summer of 1949. The stories featured in chapters four and five of *Erased* are as complex as any movie from that era, yet are not the work of Raymond Chandler, James Ellroy, or Humphrey Bogart at all, but real-life mysteries, featuring unfathomable twists, glamourous femme fatales, and even a famous movie star. These sagas, which caused a sensation at the time, are largely forgotten now. However, the stories surrounding the mysterious disappearance of a wealthy socialite, and of a budding movie star are worthy of their own Hollywood movie, and remain as dark and impenetrable now as they were in 1949.

By the summer of that year the female population of Los Angeles at last felt a little safer in their beds at night. It had now been more than two years since the slashed and dismembered body of 23-year-old Elizabeth Short had been discovered in a vacant lot on the west side of South Norton Ave in Leimert Park, Los Angeles. Although the L.A. Police Department had questioned more than 150 suspects, the murderer had never been uncovered. The brutal slaying of real estate agent Gladys Kern in 1948 did create another temporary panic, as newspapers once again speculated that the killer of Elizabeth Short may have resurfaced. However, by the summer of 1949 it seemed that social barriers had once again been dropped, and normal lives resumed without fear.

Mimi Boomhower

For well-known and apparently wealthy socialite Emily Edith Ann Luhan Boomhower (known to her friends as Mimi), life continued very much as normal. Mimi was frequently seen at the most fashionable Hollywood nightclubs and cocktail bars, organised regular dinner parties, and attended the city's most prestigious galas and fundraisers. Although born in 1896, when the occasion demanded, Mimi gave her age as forty-eight and not fifty-three.

In the early years of their marriage, during the late 1920s and early 1930s, Mimi and her late husband had spent time travelling from their New York home on long safaris to East Africa. After settling in Bel-Air, California, in middle age, the couple enjoyed the glamour of Hollywood, eating in restaurants on Sunset Strip, visiting movie theaters, and mixing with the glamorous movie stars of the era. However, just like the silver screen, there was to be an unexpected plot twist in their story as fate stuck out a foot and tripped up Mimi.

Mimi's husband, millionaire linoleum magnate and big game hunter Novice Boomhower, had passed away six years earlier, in 1943. His death was sudden and unexpected, leaving Mimi heartbroken. He was fifty-eight at the time and several years Mimi's senior. Novice Boomhower had left Mimi as the sole beneficiary of his fortune and the couple's ten-bedroom Spanish style mansion at 701 Nimes Road in Bel-Air. To outsiders, it seemed that Mimi's bread was buttered on both sides. Her expensive jewellery, large house, extravagant and ostentatious lifestyle, perhaps attracted envious eyes.

Nevertheless, despite her publicly lavish lifestyle, Mimi appeared to be undergoing some private financial difficulties and had been secretly attempting to sell her assets while simultaneously raising funds elsewhere. In February 1949 she had negotiated an equity loan, in order to start her own business as a manufacturer of wooden garden furniture. Despite cashing in the equity loan cheque for $5,000 (approximately $60,000 today), the business never actually commenced trading. In addition, Mimi had begun discreetly pawning her late husband's possessions including his hunting trophies and a watch valued at $3,000 (for which she seemed happy to be accept only a derisory $100). In the spring of 1949, her terracotta-tiled Bel-Air mansion was placed on the market for $65,000, despite the real estate agent valuing the mansion at $75,000 (equivalent to $900,000 today). It seemed that Mimi required a quick sale. Yet, despite her apparently urgent need for quick and ready cash, she still attended several lavish and expensive Hollywood society functions during the first half of 1949, and always wore her valuable collection of jewellery, estimated to be worth $25,000 (more than $300,000 today). Outwardly, her life appeared to continue as it had for many years. She may not have been on skid-row yet, publicly at least, but something had happened to cause Mimi Boomhower great concern.

On the anniversary of her husband's death (Wednesday August 17th 1949), Mimi traditionally dined with her good friend, Stella Hunter. However, that night, shortly before the pair were due to meet, Mimi called Stella and cancelled:

'Stella, I'm terribly sorry, my dear, but I simply can't have dinner with you tonight. Something important has come up.'

Mimi was polite, and always punctual. If she was ever forced to cancel an engagement, she would always telephone first to apologise. Unfortunately, on this occasion she did not elaborate regarding the *'something important'* to her friend, Stella.

The following morning, Thursday August 18th, Mimi called on her business manager and friend, Carl Manugh. He had moved to Los Angeles from Kansas City and established himself as a real estate agent and building contractor. Throughout the course of 1949 he had been a frequent visitor to Mimi's mansion in Bel-Air.

That afternoon, during her visit to Manugh's office, Mimi informed him that she was expecting a gentleman to call at her house around 8pm that evening. She promised to telephone Manugh around 8.30pm and let him know how the meeting went. Manugh assumed the gentleman to be a prospective buyer, interested in purchasing Mimi's house, and that the man must had made an appointment to view the property (although 8.30pm did seem an unusual time to arrange a home viewing). Mimi did not reveal the man's name.

Following her afternoon appointment with Carl Manugh, she returned alone to her Bel-Air mansion. At just after 7pm, Mimi received a telephone call from another friend, Helen Taylor. It was the third phone conversation between the pair that day, during which they excitedly discussed a party to be held at a San Gabriel Valley Ranch on the following Sunday, August 21st. Some of their conversation had revolved around a Los Angeles real estate agent named Fred McColloch. Mimi had met him on several occasions and appeared to enjoy his company. Her easy and friendly manner, not to mention her outward appearance of wealth, had helped Mimi garner many male admirers. She enjoyed socialising and was known affectionately as 'the Merry Widow', although Mimi – at least according to her friends – had shown no interest in a serious romance since the death of her husband.

During her telephone conversation with Helen Taylor, Mimi confided in her friend,

'Helen, I've just been out with Fred and met his mother. He's such a nice fellow.'

Helen asked to meet him, to which Mimi replied,

'How about having a party next week, then?'

Their call ended around 8 pm. Mimi then changed her dress, placing the outfit she had been wearing during the earlier part of the day onto her bed (presumably to be returned to her wardrobe later), and picked up her white leather purse. She also prepared a salad, which she then carried from the kitchen, through to the dining room table.

Mimi did not telephone her business manager at 8.30 pm, as she had promised. Manugh made several attempts to reach her by phone, both that evening and the following day (Friday August 19th), however his telephone calls went unanswered. Mimi's good friend

Stella Hunter also tried to call on both Friday 19th and Saturday 20th, but without success.

On Saturday evening, a neighbour, Mrs Muirhead, noticed that several lights had been left switched on in the Boomhower mansion, the light was clearly noticeable, bleeding through the cracks in the drapes. Unusually, the outdoor lights, mounted on the walls surrounding the patio, and those next to the garage, had also been left switched on, since at least Thursday evening. She also tried to phone Mimi's home without success. Worried about her neighbour, Mrs Muirhead eventually went across the street and rang the bell twice. She even tossed pebbles at the bedroom window to attract Mimi's attention, but to no avail. Only a dead silence emanated from the apparently empty house.

Mimi's Bel-Air Mansion

Mrs Muirhead wondered whether she should contact the police or not; but eventually decided against it. Perhaps she was comforted by the fact that the patrol cars of the Bel-Air Patrol, a private security guard agency, continually cruised the streets of that particular wealthy Bel-Air district throughout the night. *'Surely, they would have reported and investigated anything unusual?',* Mrs Muirhead thought to herself. This thought allayed any immediate fears she had for Mimi Boomhower, and she eventually decided against contacting the police.

During the 1940s the trees and bushes surrounding the properties on Nimes Road were a good deal less established than they appear today, making it easier for Mimi's neighbours to observe her home. However, unknown to the neighbour Mrs Muirhead, the security guards from the Bel-Air Patrol had also noticed the lights burning continuously from Mimi Boomhower's mansion as they drove around the bend in the road. Unfortunately, they had ignored it, simply assuming that Mimi had employed the usual tactic of wealthy Bel-Air residents, of choosing to leave their lights switched on while vacationing, in order to deter intruders.

That same evening, Saturday August 20th, Mimi had a previously arranged dinner date with Fred McColloch, however, she did not arrive at the Sunset Strip restaurant at the agreed time. Puzzled, and knowing this to be out of character for Mimi, Fred McColloch phoned her several times but could not get through. He finally decided to call Mimi's friend Stella Hunter, and the pair drove to Mimi's house together at 10pm. They, too, noticed that several lights were still burning, and a newspaper dated 'Friday 19th August' lay undisturbed on the doorstep. The front door was locked, so the worried pair walked around to the walled garden and tried the rear door, which was also secured. Fred McColloch noticed that Mimi's car was still in the garage. However, there were no indications of a break-in or a disturbance, nor of anything out of place, so the pair left, perplexed and uneasy.

On the morning of Sunday August 21st, still unable to reach Mimi, Fred McColloch and Stella Hunter finally decided to call the Westwood police station, in West Los Angeles, and report their concerns. Hard-boiled Detective Jack Ferges from the L.A. Detective Bureau was assigned to the case and accompanied the pair to Mimi's Bel-Air home at midday. They found the door still locked but, using a passkey obtained from the private security agency, obtained access. Detective Ferges, together with Stella Hunter and Fred McColloch, searched the house from top to bottom. There was no sign of Mimi. The house was tidy, with no sign of any forced entry or of a robbery. In fact, nothing seemed out of the ordinary. Mimi's discarded dress still lay on the bed, the uneaten salad on the dining-room table, the lights still on, and her car in the garage. It was as if Mimi had just stepped outside for a moment.

Detective Ferges wondered about Mimi's expensive jewellery collection. They searched the house again and confirmed that her jewellery was not there. *'That doesn't necessarily mean they've been stolen,'* Stella Hunter informed the detective, *'She may be wearing* *them. Mimi never went out without wearing her diamonds. Even her $5,000 diamond ring.'*

With no sign of Mimi, but also with no indication that any crime had actually been committed, police officers were unsure how to proceed. Mim's keys were also not present, which seemed to reinforce the notion that she had left the house of her own free will, locking the door behind her, and taking her keys with her. Nevertheless, Fred McColloch and Stella Hunter managed to convince Detective Ferges that a sudden, unexplained disappearance of this nature was so out of character for Mimi, that something must be wrong. As a result, a formal investigation was launched. Neighbours were questioned, and a description with accompanying photograph was released to the papers.

An appeal was published in several Californian papers on the morning of Tuesday August 23rd 1949, with a number of editors choosing to unfairly embellish their description of Mimi,

'Missing: Mimi Boomhower, widow, aged 48. Short, a little stout in appearance, with jet black hair which is exquisitely coiffed, black eyes, expensive clothes and jewellery.'

She was also, rather unfairly, described by various newspapers as *'raven-tressed and plump'*, *'the diamond-decked merry widow'* and *'plump and prominent.'*

Of course, the Los Angeles press sensationalised their coverage of the story, hinting at intrigue or a sexual scandal. In the film noir era, where women were portrayed in movies as secretive, furtive, and manipulative, it is perhaps understandable that the press might automatically attach some intrigue and suspicion to Mimi's disappearance; with some newspapers even suggesting she was the architect of her own downfall. Pictures such as *A Woman's Secret, Double Indemnity,* and *To Have and Have Not,* no doubt confirmed this stereotype. Somehow, the public were led to believe, Mimi must be mixed up in something.

Meanwhile, the L.A Police began their investigation in earnest.

Detectives dusted the mansion for fingerprints, however they were able to eliminate all the prints they uncovered, as belonging to either Mimi, her part-time maid and gardener, or various friends. All of these individuals were eliminated from the investigation; and were not suspected of any crime. At that moment, of course, there was still no proof that a crime had in fact been committed. Police sniffer dogs were given Mimi's scent from the dress she had left laid out on her bed, but were unable to detect her trial leading in any direction from the house, probably meaning she had left by car.

Several of Mimi's associates told Detective Ferges that she had mentioned the idea of taking a trip to a health resort on a ranch near the city of Tecate, in Baja California, just across the border in Mexico. Stella Hunter reported that,

'She sent word not to worry if she vanished for a while because she was thinking of going to some reducing ranch or home.'

Officers did find several leaflets for the Rancho La Puerta health resort in Tecate scattered about Mimi's house. A visit to a Mexican health farm was a very fashionable pastime for well-off Californian ladies in the 1940s and many such resorts had sprung up across the border. Even today many still thrive, including the Rancho La Puerta, although, whether Mimi ever actually reached there still remains shrouded in mystery. The police contacted Edmond Bordeaux Szekely, the founder of the Rancho La Puerta ranch, however, he had welcomed no resident of that name since the date of Mimi's disappearance. It was thought possible that she may have checked in under a pseudonym, however no concrete evidence could be unearthed to prove this, and the line of enquiry was eventually dropped.

Rancho La Puerta, Tecate, Mexico

Her friend Stella Hunter remained convinced that spontaneous decisions, such as suddenly disappearing to a health resort, were abnormal behaviour for Mimi, who was a careful planner with a conversative personality, not prone to such off-the-cuff whims of fancy. She also had several engagements already planned for the week following her disappearance, which her friends were convinced she would have politely cancelled if she had really booked a vacation. Besides, Mimi's refrigerator was fully stocked, all the lights had been left switched on, and her 1941 Plymouth Sedan was still in the garage.

Next, detectives contacted local taxicab firms, however no one had a record of a pickup from Bel-Air that evening. It also appeared that Mimi had ordered several items from local stores, which were duly delivered in the days following her strange disappearance, hardly the actions of someone about to leave on vacation.

Next, Detective Ferges found a mysterious postcard in Mimi's mailbox. The postcard had been franked and mailed from Long Island City, in Queens, New York, and contained just six words:

'Olga gave me your news — Lillian'

Mimi did have a sister named Olga Herman. However, Olga did not know anyone named Lillian, and wasn't aware that Mimi did either. None of her friends could recollect Mimi ever mentioning anyone called Lillian, or that Mimi knew anyone from Long Island City (other than her sister Olga). More mysteriously still, Mimi's sister claimed to have no idea what 'news' the postcard was referring to.

The police also questioned Mimi's part-time gardener, who worked for two days a week at the mansion.

'For about a week before Mrs Boomhower went away,' he told Detective Ferges, *'a white-haired, middle-aged man sat in an expensive car on the next driveway. He kept watching the place.'*

All efforts to trace this man failed, and no one came forward to identify themselves as that particular person of interest. Eventually the police assumed he was merely another realtor interested in buying or selling Mimi's property and dropped this line of enquiry too.

Part Two:

On Wednesday August 24th, a man telephoned the Los Angeles Police Department's Missing Persons' Bureau. Even by 1949, this specialist bureau had been in existence for a number of years, due to the alarming increase in the number of individuals reported missing.

The man, who was a retired police officer told the bureau:

'I'm an old-time officer myself and this is straight dope. I saw Mimi Boomhower last Thursday night (the last day on which there had been as confirmed sighting of her) *in the cocktail bar of the Roosevelt Hotel with Tom Evans, the Las Vegas gambler.'*

The call piqued the detectives' interest and they questioned Tom Evans at length. Thomas E. Evans was an ex-employee of Tony "The Hat" Cornero, a bootlegger and casino operator, and he was well-known to the police. Evans had acted as a host on one of Tony Cornero's boisterous floating casino ships that dotted the Pacific waters off Los Angeles, just outside the international waters limit, at which point state gambling legislation could not be enforced. Evans was also known by the police to be an associate of infamous L.A. mobster Mickey Cohen, who famously drove around the city in his bulletproof car.

Hollywood Roosevelt Hotel

Tom Evan told the investigating officers that,

'Sure, I was in the bar at the hotel. I go there every day. But I wasn't with this Mrs Boomhower. I never even heard her name until it got in the papers.'

Detectives considered Tom Evans a strong 'person of interest' in Mimi's disappearance, with many people convinced that Mimi had developed a gambling addiction (which may have explained why her late husband's fortune seems to have evaporated so quickly). Indeed, there was some speculation that she may have run up debts with a mobster gambling syndicate who, in return, had wanted Mimi to sign over her Bel-Air mansion to them (which they intended to convert into a gambling palace). Did they become angry and dispose of Mimi when she refused? It was certainly thought to be a strong possibility; however, this line of enquiry was also dropped due to a lack of any real evidence.

Interestingly, the name of Tom Evans would resurface in another police investigation a few weeks later; in a case that potentially may have been linked to the disappearance of Mimi Boomhower.

In an attempt to create a timeline, the police began tracking Mimi's movements in the days and weeks prior to her disappearance. They soon discovered that Mimi had visited her Beverly Hills furrier William Marco to purchase a new minx coat. When Mr Marco had pressed her for the order, Mimi had replied, *'I can't give you an order now because I'll have to talk it over with my husband.'* According to Mr Marco, she had then quickly corrected herself, adding, *'I mean. I'll talk it over with my family and come back.'*

The remarks seemed significant to the investigators. Had Mimi secretly married or eloped and not wanted to tell her friends? In her comment, Mimi had referred to talking the matter over '*with my family.*' Yet, Mimi had no children and Novice had passed away in 1943. In fact, she had no relatives at all in the Los Angeles area. Her three brothers and two sisters all lived thousands of miles away on the other side of the country. What did her remark *'I'll talk it over with my family'* really mean?

Mimi's nearest sibling was her sister Olga (her name had been mentioned in the postcard left in Mimi's mailbox). Olga lived with her husband Earle in Hewlett, Long Island, some 3,000 miles away. To assist in clearing up the mystery of the puzzling postcard, Olga and her husband were invited to California by Detective Ferges. After a gruelling nineteen-hour flight from Newark, Olga was taken straight to Bel-Air by investigators and asked to carefully cast her eye over the mansion to look for anything that seemed out of place. This she did. According to Olga nothing seemed to be missing, other than Mimi's jewellery, which she usually wore anyway. Mimi's personal papers and documents revealed nothing, and there were no indications in the house to suggest that Mimi had eloped or was intimately involved with a new lover.

Olga stood outside Mimi's mansion and addressed the waiting newspaper reporters with a grave tone, as if she knew beyond a shadow of a doubt, that something was very wrong:

'Mimi talked about taking a vacation, but it wasn't her habit to break any appointments without notifying someone. She was in good health and happy. I have found nothing here to help us find her. Absolutely nothing. My husband and I have discarded every theory for Mimi's disappearance except foul play.'

The case seemed to be becoming more unfathomable with every passing day.

Finally, on Thursday August 25th, a full week after her disappearance, the first breakthrough came in the case, for the beleaguered police department. Harry Kanaga, the manager of an upmarket grocery store at 9331 Wilshire Boulevard, close to the junction with South Elm Drive, and approximately four miles from Mimi's home, telephoned Detective Ferges urging him to *'Please ome over here at once.'* Investigators arrived at the store to be met by an excited Mr Kangaga, who immediately escorted the officers to one of the telephone booths at the back of the store. Inside was a white calfskin purse. Inside the purse were Mimi's bank card, some cash, her house and car keys, her driving licence, lipstick, and her make-up compact. Nothing appeared to be missing. Even more mysteriously, on the side of the purse, shakily written in an ink pen directly onto the white calfskin, were the words:

'Police Dept – we found this at the beach Thursday night.'

There could be no doubt the purse belonged to Mimi. It was recognised by an old friend of Mimi's late husband, George Wurzburger, who had photographed her holding the purse just a week earlier. He was also able to confirm to the police that the handwriting was not Mimi's.

No one at the store could remember anyone leaving the purse, nor acting suspiciously around the store's phone booths.

As a precaution a search was ordered of the ocean and shoreline from Malibu to Palos Verdes, however no further clues were forthcoming.

The Photograph of Mimi's purse, issued by the Police to all newspapers.

Meanwhile, the purse was sent to the Los Angeles Police Department Crime Laboratory to be examined. Despite the writer of the message claiming that that they had found the purse 'at the beach', there were no indication of saltwater damage, watermarks, sand on the inside or the outside of the purse, nor any discernible fingerprints.

Either the finder of the purse did not wish the police to know where they had really found it; or they knew a great deal more than they had claimed. The discovery simply raised yet more questions, yet frustratingly provided no answers. Had the purse really been driven the twelves miles or so inland from the beachfront to the grocery store; and by whom? Had they driven along Santa Monica Boulevard (the quickest direct route from the coast) and, if so, were they witnessed by anyone else? Or, had the purse actually been found elsewhere? And why leave it at a grocery store? Whichever assumption was true, Detective Ferges still had no answer to three even more important questions – why did the finder not wish to reveal themselves, what had been the true location of the purse, and did its discovery mean that Mimi might still be alive?

An appeal by the police for more information proved fruitless, however. No one came forward and this line of investigation, although seemingly crucial, proved to be yet another dead end. Eventually, any hopes of locating the person who had carefully placed the purse in the phone booth slowly ebbed away.

Frustrated with their lack of progress, the police decided to re-investigate Mimi's financial affairs.

It appeared that Mimi had been attempting to sell her furnishings, together with many of her late husband's big game trophies from their various East African safaris. The large collection was reputed to be worth as much as $300,000 (approximately $3.7 million today). She had made several representations to dealers in *objet d'art* hoping to offload some of the larger trophies, elephant tusks, and animal skins. Mimi had even indicated that she was prepared to accept a fraction of their value for a quick sale. It seems her outward displays of wealth were in marked contrast to her actual financial situation. While her diary was crammed with extravagant social activities, her jewellery boxes full, and her closets laden with expensive clothes; Mimi's six bank accounts were all but empty. She had also managed to persuade a West Los Angeles bank to grant her a remortgage loan of $5,000 against the value of her Bel-Air home. In fact, it seems that she had intended to cash the cheque the following week. Perplexingly, in yet another mystery, this cheque was never cashed. Furthermore, a year earlier, another loan against the property's value had been granted by Mimi's bank, but never actually taken up. Mimi's need to raise substantial sums of money seems to have been a longstanding necessity.

In July of 1949, a month before her disappearance, Mimi had offered her diamond watch to the Beverly Hills Loan Company, telling the proprietor Julius Zimmelman that she wished to be, *'relieved of it in return for a little cash.'*

He expertly examined the watch, and stated that, *'the watch is 20 to 25 years old, carries 127 diamond chips, and has a wholesale value of $200 or possibly $300.'*

He offered Mimi $100, with which she seemed quite satisfied. Mimi took the $100, confidently stating, *'I'll be back soon to pick up the watch'.*

As she turned to leave, Mimi added, *'Then I may sell you this….'*

Novice Boomhower's African trophy collection

Instead of finishing her sentence, Mimi simply flashed her diamond ring to Mr Zimmelman, who took out his loupe and closely examined the extravagant adornment to her finger.

'It's heavily insured,' Mimi explained.

'Oh, you wouldn't put up much of a fight if someone tried to take it away from you, then?', Mr Zimmelman joked.

No, I guess not.' Mimi replied, apparently in high spirits.

Was there a certain sad irony in Julius Zimmelman's words? He never saw Mimi Boomhower again, who failed to ever return and collect her beloved watch.

After Detective Ferges had interviewed her friend and neighbour, Mrs Muirhead, two more anomalies in Mimi's life surfaced. Firstly, it appeared that, despite appearing carefree and fun-loving on the exterior, another side to Mimi's character lingered below the surface. In a recent conversation with her neighbour, Mimi had claimed that,

'I'm not the scared type. I haven't known fear since my 1930 safari in Africa when me and my husband shot charging bull elephants and rhinoceroses',

Yet, she also seemed to suffer from autophobia - the fear of being alone – especially at home.

According to Mrs Muirhead, *'Mrs Boomhower often insisted on me accompanying her into her empty house at night. To satisfy Mimi, I looked under beds and in closets just in case someone was there.'*

Secondly, Mrs Muirhead told Detective Ferges that Mimi's approach to safeguarding her valuables appeared to have changed significantly in the previous three or four years. While, previously, she had not taken any particular precautions with her jewellery and had even laughed off the accidental loss of a large emerald ring and string of pearls, she had lately taken a much more responsible attitude to such valuable possessions. Either locking them in a strongbox or choosing to wear them continuously, rather than leaving them in an empty house. Such was the veracity of her newfound fiscal responsibility that in late 1945 she had suddenly decided to make a will – an act completely out of character for the fun-loving 'Merry Widow'. Detective Ferges decided to interview Mimi's lawyer, Mr H.H. Holman.

He was able to shed some light on both Mimi's financial position and her state of mind,

'Mrs Boomhower made a will in December 1945 and at that time the value of her property and personal effects was $250,000 (equivalent to approximately $4.2 million today), *Now it is much less. She was, naturally, concerned about her financial situation but was not depressed. She wasn't bankrupt.*

In the interim, Mimi's bank in West Los Angeles feared that a protracted delay in locating her whereabouts would result in a default on mortgage repayments, and promptly threatened to foreclose on the property. Obviously, Mimi's financial situation was more precarious than it had outwardly appeared. Her bank's intimate knowledge of her affairs had clearly led them to assume that her disappearance was financially related and would result in her failing to maintain her mortgage payments. At this point only a week had passed since Mimi's disappearance.

Meanwhile, Mimi's sister Olga had attempted to redeem the diamond-encrusted watch from the Beverly Hills Loan Company. However, the proprietor Mr Zimmelman informed Olga that the watch could not be returned to anyone except the owner, without the correct legal papers or a court-mandated document declaring that individual to be legally dead.

Thus, on August 29th, just eleven days after Mimi's disappearance, her lawyer Mr H.H. Holman appealed to the Los Angeles County Court. The pronouncement of Superior Court Judge Newcomb Condee caused a mild sensation at the time,

'Under California law it is not possible for me to declare a missing person dead for at least 90 days after their disappearance. But I will waive this law because of the urgency of the situation, so you may administer this shrunken estate.'

And so, just eleven days after the last confirmed sighting of Mimi Boomhower, she was declared legally dead. One perplexed L.A. County official exclaimed, *'Some folks are on vacation for longer than that! Imagine coming home from an impromptu trip, without telling anyone, to find out you were dead, all your possessions were gone, and the bank had the keys to your front door!'*

Thickset Deputy Chief of Police, Thad Brown, was forced to stand on the steps of the police precinct with a face like thunder and explain the Police Department's position to the waiting newshounds, *'Hey! We never said Mrs Boomhower was dead. We simply don't know what happened to her.'* And, in line taken straight from the movie *Farewell My Lovely*, he added, *'Don't forgot how big this city is!'*

The ludicrous nature of this situation was highlighted when several lawyers informed Judge Condee that his legal declaration of Mimi's death had been completely pointless, since California loan companies were required by law to hold all pawned articles for six months before disposing of them. In addition, he could have allowed a limited sale of her assets without the need to have her declared legally dead.

The whole affair seemed a messy business; even having the appearance of farce, which certainly did not help the investigation into Mimi's disappearance. Eventually, three months later and under mounting criticism, Judge Condee was forced to reverse his decision and restore the status of 'legal life' to Mimi Boomhower. The judge admitted he had been mistaken and stated *that 'there was lack of proof that Mrs Mimi Boomhower was dead.'*

He also rescinded the appointment of Mr H.H. Holman as administrator of Mimi's estate and granted Olga Herman's special plea, as Mimi's nearest surviving relative, to be a named trustee. Judge Condee also granted a special dispensation to allow the sale of Mimi's late husband's valuable African game trophy collection. This was permitted by the courts in order that it might help raise enough funds to pay off the $5,800 now outstanding in mortgage repayments on Mimi's Bel-Air mansion. Mimi's sister and lawyer had hoped that the trophy sale might generate as much as $200,000 towards her outstanding debts; however, the final figure achieved by the auction fell a long way short of that target. The single largest purchase was made by a gentleman named John M. Schilesser, who paid $4,500 (approximately $55,000 today) for an African elephant's head, stuffed, and complete with its impressive seven-foot tusks. However, on returning home with the item, Mr Schilesser discovered that the elephant's tusks had been cunningly replaced with over 175 pounds of plaster of Paris. It seems that Mimi's financial difficulties may have been a reality for a great deal longer than originally suspected.

The idea that Mimi's pecuniary state was so precarious, she has been forced to switch th valuable ivory for plaster, hints at two theories not properly explored by the police during the initial investigation. Firstly, obviously her financial situation had been more perilous and long-standing than anyone knew at the time. Secondly, and most importantly of all, perhaps Mimi was a great deal more devious and cunning than anyone had realised. This opened up many more intriguing theories to explain her mysterious disappearance (which will be explored later).

During the weeks that followed Mimi's disappearance, the lack of developments in the investigation gradually saw both the public and the police lose interest in the case. In less than a month the story had slipped from the pages of the newspapers altogether. Then, dramatically, just six weeks after Mimi's mysterious disappearance, a new and even more sensational headline hit the country's front pages. This time the story had everything that the scandal-obsessed public craved – a beautiful, young woman, the promise of romantic intrigue, mystery, and above all, a hint of Hollywood glamour (which will be explored in *Erased Chapter 5: The Dancer Who Disappeared*), Mimi's story, like Mimi herself, simply evaporated; forgotten and discarded.

The new saga, however, seemed to have several chilling parallels to the mysterious disappearance of Mimi Boomhower. Perhaps both women had met the same fate? Had the murderer of Elizabeth Short, dubbed the Black Dahlia Killer, returned once again? Was another serial murderer on the loose in the City of Angels? Just like the plot of the film noir classic *Laura*, starring the glamourous Gene Tiernay, the public simply lapped it up.

Of all the possible theories to explain the disappearance of both women, the most sensational (and therefore the one most likely to sell newspapers) was the possible return of Elizabeth Short's unknown killer. Her brutal murder in January 1947 still sent a shiver down the spine of any lone woman walking the streets of Los Angeles at night, or receiving an unexpected knock at the door,

Soon, among the female population of the city, a wave of hysterical fear swelled. Newspapers all asked the same question,

'Is the unknown murderer of Elizabeth Short on the prowl again?'

Part Three:

If such a vicious killer was indeed active, the Los Angeles Police Department could not afford to be complacent. This time they much the killer.

The body of 23-year-old Elizbeth Short, dubbed '*The Black Dahlia*' by the press, had been found in the Leimert Park neighbourhood of the city during January 1947; at that time a largely undeveloped area offering the killer ample opportunity to dispose of her body without being disturbed.

Elizabeth Short's face had been slashed from ear to ear, then washed by the killer (presumably to remove any forensic evidence), and finally severed in two at the waist. Police had only been able to identify the body from Short's fingerprints, on file from her arrest three years earlier on a charge of underage drinking.

The case, which was hugely sensationalised by the press, has become one of the most notorious and brutal unsolved murders in history.

Could the disappearance of Mimi Boomhower really mean the Black Dahlia killer had resurfaced? If he was at large again then, this time, he had managed to dispose of Mimi's body secretly and without leaving any clues.

Surely, the *L.A Times* conjectured (when referring to the second disappearance, a few weeks after Mimi's),

'If two attractive brunettes have mysteriously vanished without a trace in the space of six weeks then the Black Dahlia killer must have returned.'

The last known photograph of Elizabeth Short, taken shortly before her murder.

The newspapers, frustrated with the lack of developments in Mimi's case, were focusing on the second disappearance by mid-October. Meanwhile, the police continued in their efforts to uncover Mimi's whereabouts. However, without any real leads, the L.A.P.D. investigation eventually stuttered to a halt, leaving a long case file listing the most probable theories to explain her disappearance, and a host of potential suspects:

Firstly, there was the very real possibility that Mimi had secretly remarried. After all, she had mentioned *'my husband'* at the Beverly Hills furrier, then quickly corrected it to *'my family'*. Detectives remembered the postcard found in Mimi's mailbox,

'Olga gave me your news — Lillian'

Did this refer to a secret marriage or a new relationship? The police thought it possible, however, Olga had already claimed to have no idea of the postcard's meaning.

Following the death of her husband six years earlier, Mimi had occasionally accepted dinner invitations from several men, but none of these appeared to be serious romances (at least, to the outside world). In fact, Mimi had told her friends that she had little interest in remarrying. Nevertheless, Mimi's slip of the tongue at the furriers had raised doubts in the minds of detectives. Conceivably, they surmised, Mimi may have secretly eloped with a new lover, thus enabling her to escape her mounting debts and begin a new life far away, perhaps even as far away as Mexico. After all, her valuable collection of jewels had not been found at her Bel-Air home probably meaning that, if Mimi had eloped, she had taken her jewellery with her. The valuable collection of diamonds would help her sustain her lavish lifestyle – at least in the short term. However, they would not support her indefinitely; and certainly not in the way she has become accustomed to. Had she rushed into a marriage for financial reasons? To use an expression often found in the movies of the period, perhaps Mimi had found herself a 'meal ticket.'

Of course, Mimi may have mentioned a fictitious husband while shopping at the furriers, simply to avoid being pressured into a sale she could ill afford. However, this seems unlikely. If Mimi really was in such a dire financial position, why was she shopping for furs in an expensive Beverly Hills boutique in the first place?

An alternative theory regarding a possible new, and unknown, husband was also considered by detectives. Had Mimi managed to convince a new lover that she was a woman of wealth, with substantial independent means. Money attracts money, especially in Hollywood. If Mimi had found herself a new and wealthy husband, perhaps he had uncovered the truth about her precarious financial position, and a furious argument had ensued. Had he either deliberately or accidently killed her, then covered up his crime? Police considered this another possibility. Such a man may not have wished to share his wealth with Mimi in the event of a divorce. Nevertheless, despite extensive enquiries, detectives could find no evidence to support this potentially sinister theory. If this had indeed been the chain of events, then the murder must have taken place away from Mimi's home, which showed no evidence of a disturbance. This line of investigation was also dropped.

The involvement of the Los Angeles mob was also closely investigated by the L.A.P.D. If Mimi had really developed an addiction to gambling, this would explain her rapidly decreasing assets. Mimi had already considered selling her late husband's African trophy collection, which was believed to be worth approximately $300,000 at the time (more than $3 million today). She seemed willing to accept far less than the collection's true worth, which tends to indicate someone with a desperate need to raise urgent funds. Was she really '*at the mercy of those little white squares that roll around and decide whether you win or lose',* to quote a line from the film *Brute Force*?

Tom E. Evans had been seen drinking cocktails with Mimi at the Hollywood Roosevelt Hotel just days before her disappearance. Evans, as associate of Tony 'the hat' Cornero, was questioned by the police but denied knowing or ever meeting Mimi. As mentioned earlier, he claimed that the first time he had ever heard the name 'Mimi Boomhower' was only when it had appeared in the newspapers. Rumours circulated widely that a gambling syndicate, possibly involving Tony Cornero, wanted Mimi's Bel-Air mansion as a front for a gambling palace. Had she really angered the mob and either gone into hiding, or been the subject of a 'hit'? The ruthless and efficient reputation of the L.A. mob would certainly account for the fact that the body of Mimi had yet to be discovered. The criminal underworld had a grizzly reputation for disposing of bodies in shallow graves, somewhere under the Californian orange groves or deep in the desert, never to be discovered.

Nevertheless, despite an ex-police officer being certain that he had witnessed Mimi with Tom E Evans, no further evidence could be unearthed to support this line of enquiry. The *L.A. Times* reported,

'The police are discounting rumours that a scar faced gambler was angry at Mrs. Boomhower for not selling him the place for a gambling palace.'

However, several police officers at that time were known to be 'on the payroll' of L.A. gangsters; causing many to doubt the thoroughness of the L.A.P.D.'s investigation.

Another possibility considered by the police was that Mimi had chosen to take her own life, perhaps through a combination of factors including her grief over her husband's death, loneliness, and her pressing financial problems.

However, detectives could find no evidence to support this theory. Mimi's large circle of friends and acquaintances were convinced that Mimi wasn't depressed and enjoyed an active and happy social life, truly earning her the affectionate nickname *'the Merry Widow'*.

Nevertheless, this didn't discount suicide as a possibility. A person's inner turmoil is not always visible, even to their closest friends. However, if Mimi had taken her own life, where was her body? She certainly hadn't driven herself to a lonely place in order to commit suicide. Mimi's car was still in the garage, no local taxi companies had a record of collecting anyone from her mansion that night. Other factors, such as a freshly made, uneaten salad being left on her dining-room table, or the lights being left switched on, did not fit with the theory of suicide. A more sinister ending to Mimi's life still seemed to be the most likely outcome.

Rich Widow Disappears From Secluded Mansion

Police Fear Murder or Suicide; Coast of California Searched for Body

From Press Dispatches

LOS ANGELES, Aug. 25 — A wealthy widow, Mrs. Mimi Boomhower, has disappeared mysteriously here and lifeguards along the Southern California coast were alerted today to search for her body on the possibility that she had been murdered or committed suicide.

The missing widow's white purse was found late yesterday in a Beverly Hills market. On it was a shakily-printed message in black ink which read:

"To Police Dept.: We found this at the beach Thursday night."

Sgt. Jack Ferguson of the West Los Angeles Detective Bureau refused to speculate about the

would begin searching the beach "just in case."

The semi-cloth bag was identified definitely as Mrs. Boomhower's because it contained her driver's license, car keys, personal effects, credit cards and other papers, Ferguson said.

An employe found the purse in a telephone booth at a fashionable market on Wilshire Boulevard. It was given to Beverly Hills police, who turned it over to

MRS. MIMI BOOMHOWER
Who was the man?

conversation with her until 8 p. m. Thursday.

"She said she was home alone and just felt like chatting," Miss

One suggestion mooted by the L.A. newspapers was the possibility of an insurance fraud. Perhaps Mimi, influenced by one of her frequent visits to the movie theaters of Hollywood Boulevard, had hatched a plan to swindle her insurance company by staging the theft of her own valuable jewellery collection. After all, with her rumoured links to members of the L.A. underworld, it certainly would not have been too difficult for Mimi to arrange a fake robbery at her mansion and then file a bogus insurance claim. Maybe the staged theft had been inspired by one of the many movies seen by Mimi, such as *Laura, The Killers,*

Double Indemnity, or *Farewell my Lovely*, and Mimi had then been double-crossed by the thieves. Perhaps she had confronted a blackmailer in a similar fashion to Joan Bennett in *The Reckless Moment*? In Tinseltown, anything was possible.

Although the possibility of a complicated insurance fraud was an intriguing one, and ready made for the movies, there was little proof to support this line of enquiry. Once again, the L.A. detectives were back to square one. They could find no evidence to back up any of their theories regarding Mimi's disappearance, which seemed to leave just one chilling alternative – Mimi must have been abducted from her own home.

Given the atmosphere in Los Angeles at that time it is not surprising that the authorities did not wish to publicly leap to this conclusion. Firstly, there was an obvious wish to avoid creating panic among the female population of the city; and secondly, with criticism of the L.A.P.D. mounting, following a series of unsolved murders and disappearances, the Chief of Police would certainly not have wished to heap yet more public pressure on the department.

The possibility of an intruder abducting or killing Mimi certainly seemed the most likely explanation given the evidence. Mimi had openly been attempting to sell her house and was regularly seen in public adorned in her valuable diamonds. It would have been comparatively easy for a thief to have gained access inside Mimi's Bel-Air mansion posing as a potential buyer. It was well-known that Mimi lived by herself. She had no children and had lived alone since the death of her husband, Novice, six years earlier. Both Mimi's housemaid and gardener were part-time, and did not live in. Had a potential housebreaker been observing the house, it would have been a relatively straightforward task to ascertain the movements of Mimi's staff. Perhaps the white-haired man witnessed parked in a car outside Mimi's house in the week preceding her disappearance was not a prospective buyer after all, but a potential thief. This might also explain why the mysterious man never came forward to rule himself out of the investigation.

There had been no sign of a disturbance at Mimi's home. The door had not been forced open. None of the neighbours had reported overhearing an argument or a commotion. Nothing was awry, nor was there any evidence of blood or a struggle. If Mimi had been taken against her will, then her abductor must have either known her, or been plausible enough to gain access to her home under a pretext; perhaps that of being a potential purchaser. This theory was strengthened by the fact that the case bore similarities to at least one (if not several) previous murders in the Los Angeles area, including the death of the Black Dahlia, Elizabeth Short, and the brutal murder one year earlier of Gladys Kern.

A real estate agent, Gladys Kern, had met a potential house buyer at her office, on Valentine's Day 1948, before apparently accompanying him to a house in the Los Feliz district. Once inside the house Gladys was stabbed and killed by the mystery man, who was described as *'sharply dressed in a New York style', 'about 50 which greying hair'* or *'curly black* hair' (an effect easily achieved with a wig). This description did seem, a least in part, to match that of the man seen parked outside Mimi's house prior to her disappearance.

When Glady was eventually found three days later, on February 17th, her body had been carefully posed on the kitchen floor. Her valuable diamond-encrusted watch had been taken from her wrist. In addition, the killer had mailed a handwritten note to the police prior to the murder, which seemed to be in a hand similar to that of the message scrawled on the side of Mimi's purse and mentioned earlier,

'Police Dept – We found this on the beach Thursday night.'

The hyphen in the note on Mimi's purse (above) was another similarity noted by handwriting experts.

The murder of Gladys Kern and the disappearance of Mimi Boomhower were also linked to several other unsolved deaths, including those of Ora Murray in 1943, Georgette Bauerdorf in 1944, Elizabeth Short (the Black Dahlia) in 1947, and Jeanne French, one month later. However, it must be remembered that in 1949 the possibility of just one person being responsible for a series of murders was not considered as probable by police as perhaps it might be today. Psychological profiling of potential murderers was still decades away. Serial killings, such as the infamous Whitechapel Murders in London, were thankfully still comparatively rare. Indeed, the term 'Serial Killer' would not be adopted for another thirty years.

Sadly, the killer (or killers) of Ora Murray, Georgette Bauerdorf, Elizabeth Short, Gladys Kern, and Jeanne

French was never apprehended, meaning that, had that person been the same one to have abducted and killed Mimi Boomhower, he was never made to answer for his crime or reveal the location of her body to the family.

Although several similarities existed in all these cases and in the story featured in the next chapter of *Erased, (Chapter 5: The Dancer Who Disappeared*), all the trails followed by the police ran cold. These cases all still remain unsolved today.

That Mimi Boomhower was abducted from her home, by someone plausible enough to gain access to her house, still seems to be the most likely chain of events in the inexplicable disappearance of Mimi Boomhower. The question haunted L.A.P.D. detective Sergeant Ferges for the remainder of his career. Mimi's sister, Olga, certainly believed that she had been targeted by someone posing as a prospective home buyer, who then took advantage of a woman on her own, stealing her jewellery and disposing of her body. No other explanation seemed possible to the majority of Mimi's family and friends.

Although the newspapers continued to occasionally report on the investigation into Mimi's disappearance, the story eventually faded from the public eye, to be replaced six weeks later by yet another puzzling mystery.

Two years later, on November 28th 1951, Mimi's Bel-Air mansion was sold under an order granted by Judge Newcomb Condee, decreeing that the sum raised be added to the missing widow's estate. Unless definite proof was obtained that Mimi was either alive or dead, the profits from the sale would be held in trust for a further five years; at which time the proceeds would be divided equally among her brothers and sisters. Following various deductions for legal costs, maintenance, and Mimi's debts, only $40,800 remained (equivalent to approximately $470,000 today); considerably less than the property's $75,000 valuation in 1949.

Although, during the intervening years, there were several unconfirmed sightings of Mimi in locations ranging from Mexico to New York, and from Canada to Seattle, none transpired to be anything more than a wild goose chase. Occasionally, a decomposing dead body would be uncovered, which would then inevitably be linked to her case, none of these ever proved to be that of Mimi. Even sporadic newspaper articles published on the first, second and tenth anniversaries of Mimi's sudden disappearance failed to yield any further information for detectives.

Mimi's lawyer, H.H. Holman, spoke publicly about the case several years later, *'I'm sure Mrs Boomhower was the victim of foul play. I've always thought that someone who saw her expensive jewellery figured her for a robbery job and that she was killed when she put up a fight.'*

Finally, seven years after her disappearance, in August of 1956, Mimi was declared legally dead, and the proceeds of her estate divided between her brothers and sisters.

Nevertheless, the case is officially still unsolved. The file remains an open one among the thousands stored in the Cold Cases Unit of the Los Angeles Police Department. Since digitalisation, a public record is also kept at the International Center for Unidentified & Missing Persons, simply marked '*2157DFCA – Mimi Boomhower. Case Classification: Missing.*' It is still hoped that the disappearance of the lady who left behind an uneaten meal, her car, and an undisturbed empty house will one day be solved.

Perhaps it is fitting to leave the final word to the detective, Sergeant Jack Ferges, who worked tirelessly on the case for many years, in a forlorn attempt to find the missing woman,

'She just vanished into thin air. We've tracked down every possible lead. We questioned 75 friends. Each one had a different idea about what happened. Some said suicide, some said foul play. Some say she simply ran away to get married. Some say she was kidnapped.

We got letters and calls every day from people offering suggestions and clues, none of them any good. We've questioned men who were reportedly seen with her. We've checked marriage license bureaus from here to Mexico, but we're still up against a brick wall. We still don't know any more than we did at the start. It's one of the most baffling cases I ever heard of.

We still consider it a missing persons case. We have no evidence that it is otherwise.

Did she elope? And, if so, why so secretly? Did she go to a health resort and die there under an assumed name? Did she upset blackmailers? Did she drown at

the beach where her bag was found? Was she the victim of robbery? Is she alive or dead? And if she is dead, where is her body?

Stir any of these theories up and take your pick.'

Detective Jack Ferges, pictured in 1951, still working on the case.

Perhaps her family and friends were able to cling onto the faint hope that Mimi simply ran away of her own free will to escape her debts, living out a happy and quiet life somewhere, in peace and complete solitude. Her dinner date on the night she vanished, Fred McColloch, later said,

'I attended a dinner party at her home on the Tuesday before she disappeared. She was under heavy nervous strain, a direct switch of temperament. She always lived under the illusion of wealth. She was always

giving parties, but when she saw she didn't have the financing to keep her standard of living from changing, maybe she got away from it all.'

Although the enigma surrounding Mimi's disappearance on that fateful day in August 1949, was never resolved, just six weeks later, in October of that year, another equally shocking sequel brought the painful memories vividly back to life. You can read the full story of another equally baffling, and real life, Hollywood mystery that carried all the hallmarks of Mimi's disappearance, in *Erased Chapter 5: The Dancer Who Disappeared.*

Scan here for extra photographs and digital versions of the images contained in this chapter

A Blog Discussing the
Mimi Boomhower
Case

A Drive Around 1940's
LA

Mimi's Missing
Persons Case File

The F.B.I.'s Official
Black Dahlia Page

The Dancer Who Disappeared

"There is no trap so deadly as the trap you set for yourself"
Raymond Chandler, *The Long Goodbye*

Part One:

Jean Elizabeth Spangler was born in a quiet, respectable neighbourhood in Seattle, Washington State, on Sunday September 2nd 1923. She enjoyed a happy upbringing, alongside her two brothers, Richard and Edward, and her sister Betsy. After the first six years of a peaceful and unremarkable childhood, Jean's family moved to Los Angeles after her father Cecil had been offered a better paid job. It was 1929, the first 'talkies' were exploding onto the silver screens of the new Downtown movie theatres, each flickering image seemingly offering impossible glamour and excitement to the young Jean. Situated just a few miles from the newly burgeoning movie studios of Hollywood, was the Benjamin Franklin High School, in which the young Jean enrolled, alongside Star Trek creator Gene Roddenberry. In later years, pupils at the school would include actress and singer Ashley Judd and musician Daryl Hall. Jean took dancing classes as well as becoming involved in amateur dramatics at her new school.

Benjamin Franklin High School appeared to be ideal, both in location and outlook, for the young Jean's growing showbusiness aspirations.

Richard, Jean, Edward and Betsy Spangler

When Jean reached the age of sixteen she became a dancer at the Earl Carroll Theatre on Sunset Boulevard and at Florentine Gardens Nightclub, on Hollywood Boulevard. Both venues attracted a mixed clientele, ranging from movie stars to gangsters, and they both enjoyed enviable reputations. Jean became an instant favourite with the customers, thanks to her warm personality and fun-loving nature. Just a decade later, however, the Florentine Gardens would become forever associated with the unsolved slaying of

Elizabeth Short, in what would become known as the Black Dahlia murder.

Similarities uncovered during that investigation in 1947 would later lead Los Angeles Police to believe that, among others, Elizabeth Short, Mimi Boomhower (featured in *The Empty House*, Chapter 4 of *Erased*), and Jean Spangler, may have all been victims of the same killer.

Post war Los Angeles became the setting for a spate of disappearances and murders, featuring attractive brunettes, which were hastily attributed by the press to the man they sensationally dubbed as 'The Black Dahlia' murderer (a name probably derived from the 1946 noir movie *The Blue Dahlia*). The mood in Los Angeles at that time very much reflected the dark atmosphere of the film noir genre, with films such as *The Blue Dahlia, Gilda, Double Indemnity* and *Criss Cross* perfectly crystallising the underlying feeling of menace that lurked behind the neon lights on Hollywood Boulevard – particularly for young women alone on the streets. The city witnessed many unsolved murders, crime was rampant, particularly organised crime, and the L.A. Police Department faced accusations of corruption. In the bars and dive-joints of the city, with their reputation for trouble, shell-shocked G.I.s, recently returned from Europe and the Far East, rubbed shoulders with gangsters, prostitutes and pimps. Meanwhile, on the surface, in true Tinseltown style, a veneer of morality and glamour attracted the rich, the respectable, the famous, and the starry-eyed hopefuls of the mid-west to the city. At the Downtown nightclubs and restaurants, these two worlds inevitably collided, as perhaps Mimi Boomhower and Jean Spangler discovered to their cost.

1940's Hollywood

While still dancing in Hollywood nightclubs during 1941, and generally enjoying the nightlife of Downtown L.A., Jean met a young businessman named Dexter Benner. She was an attractive, bubbly, outgoing 18-year-old, with hair as dark as the dead of night; he was a sensible, quiet, strait-laced 23-year-old. Had they watched the movie *The Postman Always Rings Twice* they might well have realised there were fifteen or twenty reasons why they shouldn't have got together; and both would probably have made a different decision that night. Their friends, too, tried to picture the young couple in love; but it did not work.

Nevertheless, like a cookie full of arsenic, the couple ignored the danger signs and began a stormy relationship, marrying a short time afterwards.

Dexter Benner

Jean filed for divorce just six months later, citing cruelty, however the couple did attempt to patch up their marriage. Jean withdrew her divorce petition and their relationship limped on for a further two years until, on April 22nd 1944, Jean gave birth to a daughter, whom the couple named Christine. However, their union remained an unhappy one. Benner was a plastics manufacturer, mature for his age, and down to earth, Jean was described as a 'party girl' who enjoyed the bright lights of Hollywood, even possibly having relationships with other men. Although clearly devoted to Christine, Jean often left Dexter to look after their daughter, while she spent long nights at a series of neon lit Downtown nightclubs, or at private parties in the Hollywood Hills. When not socialising she zealously pursued her showbusiness ambitions, not the natural state of a marriage in 1940s America. Their separate lives, together with disagreements over raising their daughter, eventually caused the couple to split in 1945 followed by divorce in 1946. The pair then became embroiled in a bitter crossfire, as they fought an acrimonious custody battle over Christine. Jean accused her ex-husband of cruelty, while he claimed in court that Jean *'preferred parties to priorities'*, and that Jean was *'a glamour girl mother.'* Unusually for the time, the courts sided with Benner (perhaps feeling he offered their young daughter a more stable home environment and a sound financial base), and he was awarded temporary custody of their daughter. Jean refused to accept the verdict of the L.A. court, however, and Benner was forced to deny his ex-wife access to see her daughter no less than twenty-three times between 1946 and 1948; with the police needing to be in attendance on several occasions.

Jean at her daughter's custody hearing

Finally, by 1948, after many years of struggling to gain recognition (and financial reward) as a dancer, Jean's career in Hollywood at last appeared to be heading in the right direction.

She moved into a cosy home in the Park La Brea residential complex, close to Wilshire Boulevard in the Miracle Mile district of the city. Next, Jean acquired an agent who arranged for her to have a professional portfolio of publicity stills taken and, through his introduction, made her movie debut as an extra in the RKO feature *The Miracle of the Bells* in 1948.

The film featured two well-known stars at the time, Fred MacMurray and Frank Sinatra, and although it was not a box office success, it did raise Jean's profile among Hollywood's movie studios, and she was offered several walk-on roles in upcoming productions.

Almost as soon as she had finished filming her scenes on *The Miracle of the Bells,* she was offered small parts as a showgirl in the Betty Davis movie *When My Baby Smiles at Me,* with the Marx Brothers in *Mummy's Dummies,* and *Chicken Every Sunday* (which also featured a ten-year-old Natalie Wood, who later died in circumstances almost as mysterious as the disappearance of Jean Spangler). The telephone then began to ring steadily at Jean's apartment, not with the ominous ring of a dark Hollywood movie like *Sorry, Wrong Number*, but joyously, with offers of work, or with anxious young men looking to date the new starlet.

Jean in Mummy's Dummies, 1948

Jean with TV gameshow host
Jack Bailey

Other small roles followed in *Wasbash Avenue* and *Champagne for Caesar* (although neither film would be released until after Jean's mysterious disappearance on October 7th 1949).

This brief period of success brought with it some welcome financial reward. Jean was able to return to court and, this time, she was awarded custody of her daughter (coincidentally, by the same judge who had prematurely declared Mimi Boomhower legally dead in the previous chapter, Judge Newcomb Condee). Jean's ex-husband was also ordered by Judge Condee to make regular monthly alimony payments to Jean. Finally, her life seemed to be heading in the direction she had hoped for. Meanwhile, Jean shared her home at 6216 Colgate Ave, Park La Brea with her mother Florence, her daughter Christine, her dogs, and occasionally her sister-in-law Sophie, who often visited. Sophie had married Jean's brother Edward;

however, he had been killed on a bombing mission in the Far East on the very last day of the war.

It was an unassuming and modest home, in a pastel-coloured block of houses close to the bend at the eastern end of Colgate Ave at the point where it becomes South Ogden Drive. Although Jean was happy there, she still dreamed of a larger home in the Hollywood Hills, a beachfront mansion in Malibu, and a successful career as a movie star.

Next came Jean's big break; she was offered two more movie roles. This time in scenes in which she would share screen time with established Hollywood Stars. Firstly, in *The Petty Girl* (known internationally as *Girl of the Year*), starring Robert Cummings and Joan Caulfield.

Cummings, who would later go on to star in Alfred Hitchcock's *Dial M For Murder*, was charmed by Jean and the pair enjoyed several pleasant conversations on set, briefly becoming good friends. Jean's scenes in *The Petty Girl* were shot in September of 1949, although the movie would not be released until 1950.

However, perhaps her pivotal opportunity came in the final week of September – just ten days before her disappearance - when she was asked to film a scene with the young Kirk Douglas in the musical drama *Young Man with a Horn*.

The movie, which also starred Lauren Bacall and Doris Day, was a critical and commercial success, and might possibly have catapulted Jean to stardom.

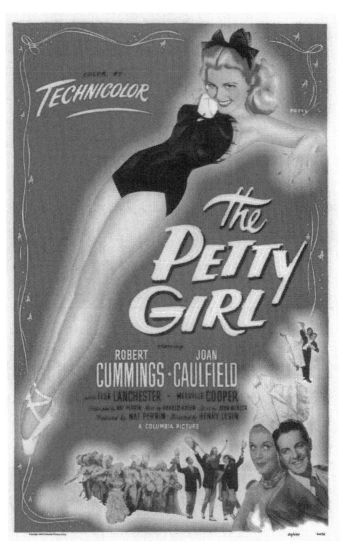

The Petty Girl was not released until several months after Jean had vanished without a trace.

Despite Jean's career seemingly moving in the right direction, and her life – outwardly at least – happy and contented, there were two dark clouds in her otherwise sunny existence. Firstly, Jean was leading a complicated private life. Like a card deck with six aces, Jean seemed to be the perfect package. Easy on the eye, tall and slender, with soft shoulders, long legs, dark hair, and ocean blue eyes, she attracted male attention easily, whether wanted or unwanted. Her naturally open manner and gregarious nature may have resulted in several men simultaneously vying for her attentions. As one newspaper would report (taking a line from the movie *Farewell My Lovely*), *'she was attracted to men; they often met her halfway.'*

Jean had recently finished a relationship with a man known as 'Scotty', whom she alleged had been abusive towards her. Despite having regained custody of her daughter, she still frequented several bars and nightclubs in the city; usually asking her mother or sister-in-law to babysit her daughter Christine. During this period of her life, it was rumoured that Jean had become acquainted with several members of the mob, including notorious L.A. gangsters Tony 'The Hat' Cornero and Mickey Cohen, at cocktail bars such as the Roosevelt Hotel on Hollywood Boulevard. Jean had certainly been seen socialising with several members of the L.A. underworld. She may have even met Mimi Boomhower and Tom Evans there (who was interviewed as a 'person of interest' by the L.A. police after Mimi Boomhower vanished without a trace). Evans would also later be questioned following Jean's unexplained disappearance.

The actor Robert Cummings, with whom Jean had struck up a friendship during the filming of *The Petty Girl*, also thought that she was having an affair with someone; probably a married man in the movie business, perhaps even someone from that film shoot, he surmised. However, he did not know the man's name.

Secondly, there still appeared to be much bad blood between Jean and her ex-husband Dexter Benner, who had by now fallen behind with his child support payments for their five-year-old daughter Christine. The couple had argued frequently until finally, in

October 1949, Jean informed her family that she had contacted Benner and demanded that he meet her in person, and discuss the issue face-to-face.

The last known photograph of Jean with her daughter Christine

Just a few days prior to Jean's disappearance, and her appointment with her ex-husband, her mother Florence decided to visit family in Lexington, Kentucky. Oddly, Florence had a strange foreboding before leaving home. She would later tell reporters,

'I told Jean, before I left, that I shouldn't go – that I had a premonition something would happen. But Jean said to me "Now, mother, I'm a big girl now and I can take care of myself." How I wish I'd never made that trip.'

While her mother was away, Jean's sister-in-law Sophie came to stay with at Colgate Ave, to babysit while Jean went out to meet her ex-husband, Dexter.

During the afternoon of Friday October 7th, Jean had suddenly announced to her sister-in-law that, *'Dexter has finally said he will meet me later this afternoon'* to discuss his outstanding child support payments. Sophie agreed to babysit Christine and, according to an interview Sophie later gave to the *L.A. Times*,

'Around 5, Jean came down the stairs and asked how she looked. She smiled at me. Then her little girl, Christine, asked where she was going. "Going to work," Jean answered again, but she winked at me when she said it.'

Jean left the house just after 5pm. It had been a pleasantly warm, dry day. The late afternoon sun was now dipping in the sky as Sophie and Jean's daughter waved goodbye. The air was now beginning to cool. Jean turned as she left, crossed her fingers in a light-hearted manner, winked at her daughter, and said,

'Well, wish me luck!'

'Good luck, mom.'

With that, Jean wrapped her fitted white coat around herself and headed north on foot, along South Ogden

Drive while her daughter waved from the doorstep and, after a few hundred yards, turned left, out of sight of her daughter, and along West 3rd Street. Here she crossed at the intersection with South Fairfax Ave, and entered the Farmers Market under the familiar clock tower. A walk of approximately five minutes.

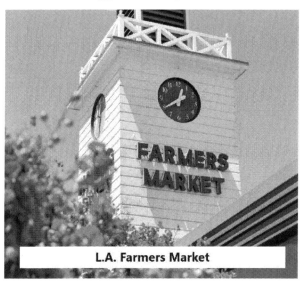

L.A. Farmers Market

Once inside the market she chatted cheerfully to Ray Miller, the proprietor of the key grinding stall. He would later put the time at around 5.30pm and told detectives that, *'I talked with her, we discussed her plans to purchase a handbag for her little girl. She seemed cheerful and in good spirits.'*

She was next seen around 6pm by Lillian Marks, the cashier at the Town and Country grocery stall inside the market. For several minutes Lillian Marks watched Jean with interest, as she seemed to be passing the time by idly browsing the displays. She thought that Jean appeared not to be shopping at all but probably waiting for someone in some pre-arranged rendezvous. Lillian Marks, who knew Jean well by sight, and through her recently acquired reputation as a budding star, was certain that no one approached Jean or spoke to her. The eagle-eyed cashier was certain of that point.

Jean stayed in full view of Lillian Marks for several minutes and she later told the police that,

'When it appeared that she'd been stood up, because I'm certain no one arrived to meet her, she eventually wandered off in the direction of the phone booths and out of my sight.'

Lillian Marks had the strong impression that Jean had arranged the Farmers Market as a suitable meeting point as she, *'probably did not wish to be picked up outside her own home; but did want to be in a public and safe place.'*

Lillian Marks also surmised that this seemed to indicate a first date of some sort, rather than a pre-arranged meeting with her ex-husband.

Around 6.00 - 6.30pm, now more than an hour since waving goodbye to her daughter, Jean phoned home (probably from a public call-booth in the Farmers' Market) and spoke to both her daughter and her sister-in-law. She did not appear to be flustered or worried in her manner, and calmly informed Sophie that she had been asked by a movie studio to work on an overnight film shoot that night, and would *'have to work the full eight hours',* adding that, *'I probably won't be back home this evening.'* Sophie would later say that Jean ended the call quickly, when a car pulled up to pick up

Jean (you can hear Sophie's interview by scanning the QR code at the end of this chapter).

Sophie was slightly surprised at her sister-in-law's sudden change of plan but, as it was now getting dark, she put Christine to bed. If Jean was away from home she usually left a telephone number, where it would be possible for her mother or sister-in-law to reach her. She had not done so this time.

Sophie retired to bed, confidently expecting to see Jean in the morning.

However, when Sophie woke on the Saturday morning Jean had still not returned. She waited a while, expecting the phone to ring at any moment, or for her sister-in-law to walk through the door. Jean would usually let her daughter know if she was working late. Jean's ex-husband Dexter frequently had custody of their daughter at weekends, and he arrived early on that Saturday morning to pick up Christine. Sophie informed him that Jean had not yet returned home from work. Dexter did not seem overly concerned and took his daughter away.

The hours then passed slowly for Sophie Spangler, alone in Colgate Ave, wondering why her sister had still not contacted her or returned to the family home. Finally, distraught with worry, she decided to call the police department. The disinterested officer on duty told Sophie not to worry, her sister-in-law would probably be home later; and did she realise who many phone calls the police department received every day informing them that someone had gone missing, only for that person to walk sheepishly through the door a few hours later.

Sophie persisted, nevertheless, and was eventually told to file a missing persons report at the Wilshire Police Station on Venice Boulevard. It seemed the only way for her concerns about Jean to be taken seriously. Several more hours had now passed and Jean had still not returned or telephoned.

Finally, at approximately 10.30pm that night – now more than twenty-four hours since Sophie had last heard from Jean – she jumped into her car and headed south, past the El Rey Theater, across Wilshire and Pico, and finally onto Venice Boulevard.

Sadly, Sophie's journey appeared to have been wasted, at least in the short term. The seemingly disinterested officer on duty informed her that overnight absences were *'many and frequent in L.A.'* Most police officers harboured a jaundiced view of those young women who had required a reputation as 'party girls' (as Jean's ex-husband had referred to Jean during their divorce). Almost every weekend, many of these so-called 'goodtime girls' were arrested for being drunk and disorderly, causing trouble, or being suspected of prostitution. They were often locked up for an overnight stop in the cells to sleep off their hangovers, only to be released the following morning to worried relatives who had already filed a missing persons report. Despite the police officer's apathy, Jean's details were routinely noted down and the report was added to the mountainous pile of case files, all detailing other missing individuals in the Downtown area. This stack of files only being dwarfed by the many reports of other worrying crimes currently facing the L.A. Police Department.

In addition to organised crime, robberies, and crimes of violence, senior officers were still at a loss to solve the recent disappearance of Mimi Boomhower from her Bel-Air mansion. Nevertheless, the two cases were not immediately linked by the police. However, when news of Jean's disappearance became public, *The L.A. Times* would hastily make the connection.

By linking the disappearance of Mimi Boomhower and Jean Spangler to the unsolved murder of Elizabeth Short two years earlier, *The L.A. Times* immediately guaranteed intense public interest in the case. Had the Black Dahlia killer struck once more? All three were attractive brunettes, one murdered, two missing, perhaps also killed? The link was an obvious one. Superficially, at least, the similarities of both previous cases, when compared to the newly reported disappearance of young and attractive brunette Jean Spangler, seemed to warrant an investigation by detectives. Sadly, however, the police did not routinely check similarities in newly filed reports against existing cases, and Jean's missing persons file was simply placed in the duty detective's in-tray, to be reviewed at some unspecified future date (or hopefully stamped 'case closed' when a red-faced Jean returned sheepishly to her family a few days later). That was the normal way of things in the hopelessly overworked L.A. County detective bureau.

Part Two:

So, Sophie returned to Colgate Ave and informed Dexter Benner that Jean had still not returned. He agreed to keep Christine. Sophie told him, *'I'll contact you if I hear anything',* and rang off. Sophie retired to bed, exhausted and troubled, hoping that the dawn of the following morning would herald some more positive news. Sure enough, the next day did bring a fresh development in the case; but it was far from the news Jean's family had been so desperately hoping for.

At 7 a.m. on that dewy Sunday morning, now more than thirty-six hours after the last confirmed sightings of Jean, a gardener named Henry Anger, who was employed by the City's Parks Department, was making his morning rounds in Griffith Park, approximately five miles from Jean's home. In an isolated area near the Fern Dell entrance to the park, close to the Observatory, he noticed something black lying in the dirt. As he approached the object, Henry Anger quickly realised it was a woman's purse. He picked it up and noticed that the ends of both straps were torn, as might occur if the purse had been ripped from a lady's hand in a bag snatch. Henry Anger looked inside the black purse, wondering if he might be able to identify the owner.

The contents would yield the first clue in the search for the missing actress. Inside, in addition to the usual female ephemera, the purse contained a packet of Lucky Strike cigarettes, a driver's license, a Screen Actors' Guild card, a Screen Extras' Guild card, brown leather address book, and a bank card, all in the of name Jean Spangler. There was no cash in the purse.

However, Henry Anger's attention was quickly drawn to a folded piece of white notepaper nestled at the bottom.

He opened it up to reveal an apparently unfinished note, written in a shaky and hurried woman's hand. The note read as follows,

'Kirk: Can't wait any longer. Going to see Dr Scott. It will work out better this way while mother is away,'

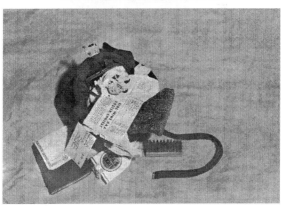

Kirk:
Can't wait any longer.
Going to see Dr. Scott.
It will work best this
way while mother is
away.

Police at the scene where Jean's purse was discovered

Henry Anger contacted the police who, at last, connected the name contained on the items in the purse with the missing persons report filed by Jean's sister-in-law. An immediate search of Griffith Park was ordered by L.A.P.D. Chief of Police William A. Worton. Detective Chief Thad Brown and Captain Harry Didion were placed in charge of the ongoing investigation.

Thad Brown had previously headed the 'Black Dahlia' murder in 1947 and had also worked on the search for Mimi Boomhower.

Griffith Park, consisted of more than 4,000 acres of landscaped ground lying just of Crystal Springs Road, and would require a huge number of officers to undertake an effective search. The case seemed to have an ominous familiarity to the weary L.A.P.D. officers – many of the men had worked on the Elizabeth Short murder - and they fully expected to find Jean's body. Ultimately, however, despite sixty police officers and as many as 200 police reservist volunteers being engaged in the search for the missing woman, their efforts proved unsuccessful. The only discovery of any note being two items of men's prison issue denims found pushed into a hole in the ground. Perhaps her attacker had been an escaped prisoner on the run who had happened upon Jean, then hidden his prison clothing. However, investigations by the police soon revealed that no prisoners had been reported as escaped or missing. The prison uniform was then passed to the L.A.P.D. Crime Laboratory; however, the items exhibited no blood traces or distinctive fibres. The clothing did not appear to be related to the disappearance of Jean Spangler.

The police theorised that the absence of any money in Jean's discarded purse might indicate a robbery gone wrong as the explanation for her disappearance. Detectives hoped that their search might led to the discovery of more items belonging to Jean, tossed away by the thief as he made his hasty getaway. Perhaps Jean had been knocked to the ground during the snatch and was lying unconscious somewhere. However, a routine conversation with Jean's sister-in-law confirmed the fact that Jean did not take any money with her on the night she vanished, probably ruling out robbery as a motive, although it may have been possible that a thief – angry at finding no cash in Jean's purse – had decided to kill her, rather than risk being identified later.

Unfortunately, a few days later, a brush fire in the Fern Dell area of Griffith Park effectively destroyed any further opportunity of obtaining additional evidence in Jean's disappearance. This fire was not officially linked to the investigation, although it timing was extremely fortuitous for anyone who may have left a telling clue to Jean's disappearance there.

Returning to the all-important handwritten note, Captain Didion sent it to Don Myre, the handwriting expert at the Los Angeles Police Crime Lab. Myre was able to compare the note with samples of Jean's handwriting taken from her home; and he confirmed that the note had indeed been written by Jean. He also observed that the writing seemed hurried, and perhaps written while upset or under emotional strain. Crucially, Myre added that the letter (which was unsigned) ended with a comma and not a full stop. He surmised that the note was unfinished, and that Jean had either been interrupted while writing it; or had most likely intended to complete it later. However, neither the note nor the other contents of the purse gave any further clue as to the identity of either Kirk or Dr Scott.

The note seemed the best clue to solving Jean Spangler's disappearance and detectives began to question her family and friends.

The name *'Kirk'* intrigued Captain Didion. None of Jean's friends recalled her ever mentioning someone of that name, however Jean's mother, Florence, remembered that somebody named Kirk had picked up Jean from the house on at least two occasions. Unfortunately, he had stayed in the car and Florence had been unable to get a clear look at him. Maybe he had not wished to be seen, Florence had thought at the time, or perhaps he was a married man. Jean had been reticent about the man too, other than telling her mother that she had met the mysterious Kirk on-set during a movie shoot. However, because of the fleeting nature of Jean's work as an extra her mother could not recall at which studio he may have worked. This left little for the police to follow up on.

Next came an extraordinary development in the search for the mysterious Kirk. Leading Hollywood actor Kirk Douglas contacted the police, entirely of his own volition, after seeing reports of the handwritten note in the newspapers. Although detectives had not officially linked Kirk Douglas with either Jean or the note, the actor wished to eliminate himself from the investigation, telling detectives that he had never met Jean and did not know her. Some speculation followed in the press, when it was revealed that Douglas had actually filmed a scene with Jean for the movie *Young Man with a Horn* only ten days prior to her disappearance. Others present on the set at the time also recalled Kirk Douglas and Jean chatting and smiling together.

Detective Chief Thad Brown re-interviewed the actor by telephone. One very obvious question was asked:

'If you didn't know her, how did you link yourself to the name "Kirk" in her note?'

Kirk Douglas with Doris Day during the filming of Young Man With A Horn

Douglas explained that he had, *'talked and kidded with her a bit on the set but didn't know her name.'*

He denied ever meeting Jean off-set and only connected her with the news of a missing actress after he had been told that Jean was the same girl who had recently filmed a scene with him. He also told Detective Chief Brown that he had been in Palm Springs on the day that Jean Spangler had disappeared.

Kirk Douglas, a rising movie star at the time, married with two small children, was understandably anxious to protect his reputation and eventually took the unprecedented step of issuing the following press statement, via his attorney Jerry Rosenthal, despite never actually being officially linked to the investigation:

'I told Detective Chief Thad Brown that I didn't remember the girl or the name, until a friend recalled that it was she who had worked as an extra in a scene with me in my picture Young Man with a Horn ... then I recalled that she was a tall girl in a green dress. I talked and kidded with her a bit on the set, as I have done with many other people. But I never saw her before or after that and have never been out with her.'
- Kirk Douglas, Oct. 12, 1949.

The police eliminated Kirk Douglas and redoubled their efforts to trace the mysterious 'Kirk', using the address book found in Jean's discarded purse, which contained the names and numbers of numerous Hollywood actors and bit-part players.

A number of Jean's friends were also re-interviewed, along with employees, crew, fellow extras, and even a number of major movie stars, employed at MGM, Paramount, Universal, 20th-Century Fox, Warners, Columbia, and RKO. The ravenous press, with a whiff of celebrity scandal in the air, and desperate to obtain the names in Jean's address book, camped outside the police precinct. Detective Chief Thad Brown would not release the names of anyone listed in Jean's address book, but instead attempted to reassure the waiting reporters by saying,

'Detectives have been assigned to check every name in the book in an effort to find the vital clue we need.' He

then rather needlessly added, *'One thing we have discovered, this girl sure got around.'*

Unfortunately, this huge logistical exercise by the police produced little. No one could recall an employee by the name of Kirk, nor remember seeing Jean in close conversation with another male extra or bit-part player. The only real clue came from actor Robert Cummings (with whom Jean had recently become friendly after filming a scene together in *The Petty Girl*), who informed the police that he thought Jean may have become involved romantically with a man she'd met at the Columbia Studios during filming. Cummings told investigators about a conversation that had taken place between Jean and himself about a week before her disappearance, in which she had cryptically suggested to him that,

'I have a new romance in my life.'

'I asked her if it was serious,' Cummings told the police. *'Jean said, "Not exactly, but I'm having the time of my life."'*

Was this the mysterious Kirk, detectives wondered? Perhaps he was already married, or even a well-known actor too afraid to use his own name?

Screenwriter Peter Brooks would later be revealed to be the new romance in Jean's life, although (according to his close friends and acquaintances) he had never used the name Kirk. Brooks, in fact, had tried to phone Jean several times both on the night she had disappeared and again the following day. Nevertheless, Brooks had a strong alibi for the night of

Jean's disappearance, and he was quickly eliminated from the police investigation.

Ultimately, the enigmatic and mysterious Kirk would never be traced.

Next, rather than concentrate their efforts on locating the shadowy Kirk, the police instead turned their attention to the cryptic contents of Jean's handwritten note - *Can't wait any longer. Going to see Dr Scott. It will work out better this way while mother is away,'*. What, exactly, was the *'it'* to which Jean referred in the note?

One of Jean's close friends informed Captain Didion that Jean was three months pregnant; and had considered having an abortion. Although none of Jean's other friends could confirm this story, it did seem to fit the wording of her unfinished note. There are two very plausible reasons which seemed to fit this theory. Firstly, it was common practice for actresses under contract to major Hollywood studios to undergo a termination, rather than risk losing a coveted role in a movie. Indeed, they were often pressured into the operation by studio executives. Many had even signed 'morality clauses' in their contracts, in which they had agreed not to become pregnant – especially when unmarried.

Secondly, perhaps Jean had been persuaded following undue pressure from the father of her unborn baby, who may have been married, or a well-known Hollywood star not wishing to be involved in a social scandal. Therefore, it is entirely plausible that Jean may have been considering an abortion. Working in an industry in which her public image and reputation meant everything, it was a completely understandable that Jean might have wished to remain tight-lipped about the whole affair.

In any event, the L.A. Police quickly became convinced that the abortion angle was the most likely explanation. The wording of Jean's note then seemed to make complete sense:

'Can't wait any longer. Going to see Dr Scott. It will work out better this way while mother is away,'

Perhaps the story about meeting her ex-husband and then working late on a film shoot was merely a ruse to explain an overnight absence from home? After all, an abortion in 1949 was an illicit procedure, that may have even required a long journey and an overnight stay. To confirm their suspicions the police decided to check out Jean's 'cover' story.

Dexter Benner and Lynn Lasky

Firstly, Captain Didion interviewed Jean's ex-husband Dexter Benner, whom Jean had told her sister-in-law she was meeting on the night of her disappearance to discuss child support payments. Although he seemed a probable suspect in Jean's disappearance, the police do not appear to have considered him one, at this point in the investigation. Benner seemed rather surprised to be find two police detectives at his front door. He claimed that he had not seen Jean for several weeks. In fact, he had remarried just four weeks previously, and had been at home all night on the day of Jean's disappearance. His new wife, Lynn Lasky Benner, corroborated his story. Benner told the officers that he was not, in fact, behind with his maintenance payments and had not agreed to meet Jean on the preceding Friday, or on any other day. This left the detectives convinced they were on the right trail; Jean's tale had been an complex cover story for a planned abortion.

Next, officers contacted every film studio Jean was known to have worked for and visited the offices of the Screen Extras Guild in Hollywood. Not only was there no record of Jean being employed on any shoot that evening; the Screen Extras Guild confirmed that no movie filming had taken place anywhere in the Los Angeles area on the night of 7th October 1949. Jean's elaborate story was clearly a fabrication.

Police officers then contacted every registered doctor by the name of 'Scott' in the Greater Los Angeles area. Despite Jean's sister-in-law not recognising the name 'Dr Scott', Captain Harry Didion stated publicly that, *'I am certain that a physician by the name of Dr Scott was known to Miss Spangler and her coterie of nightclubbing friends.'* However, in spite of exhaustive enquiries, the police were unable to locate any doctor who admitted to knowing Jean Spangler.

Hardly surprising, since abortion was mostly illegal in 1949; although there were some loopholes under which doctors were still allowed to perform the procedure, such as the mental and physical wellbeing of the mother, possible birth defects in the child, etc. Interestingly, these legal loopholes would be substantially tightened in 1950, perhaps meaning Jean Spangler's life might have taken an entirely different path had the events of October 1949 happened just a few months later. However, as the procedure was still considered an unlawful act in 1949 (both for the person performing the operation and the woman seeking it), it is far more likely that the doctor in question had used a false name under which to offer his illicit services. There had been rumours of an active ring of abortion practitioners operating in Hollywood at that time, offering the procedure to the rich and famous. Had Jean been the victim of a botched abortion, died, and her body then been buried somewhere? Realistically, no L.A. doctor was likely to come forward and admit to being the 'Dr Scott' mentioned in Jean's note, thereby risking prosecution, public disgrace, and possible imprisonment. Without a body, the abortion angle would be a near impossible one for the police to prove.

Nevertheless, an anonymous tip given to the L.A.P.D. mentioned a man known only by the name 'Doc' who apparently visited the same nightclubs and bars as Jean. Rumours had circulated in Hollywood that 'Doc' was willing to perform illegal abortions, with no questions asked. Was 'Doc' the same 'Dr Scott' referred to in Jean's hurried and unfinished note? While detectives were able to establish that the elusive 'Doc' was probably an ex-medical student and from a wealthy Californian family, they were never able to trace him.

Although the botched abortion theory seemed a highly credible one, it did not explain how or why Jean's purse had been discarded in Griffith Park, with the incriminating note still inside. If Jean had really died during a failed abortion procedure, why not simply bury her purse alongside her body? Why risk being seen disposing of the purse separately, and thereby effectively doubling the risk of being observed? And why not search the purse first and remove any possible clues linking a 'Dr Scott', or a possible termination, to Jean's disappearance? These basic errors seemed improbable in anyone intelligent and calculating enough to operate a successful and covert abortion ring.

Without any further leads being generated, that line of enquiry eventually fizzled out.

However, detectives did remember that Jean's friends had referred to her having a past relationship with someone she had referred to as 'Scotty'. Was he the mysterious Dr Scott? It was believed by Jean's friends that she had been involved with a Lieutenant in the Army Air Corp during the war, while her husband Dexter had been stationed overseas, although she had remained tight-lipped over the affair. Jean had claimed that 'Scotty' had been abusive towards her; threatening to kill her when she had attempted to end their relationship in 1945. Although the police thought the jilted Lieutenant was almost certainly the 'Scotty' she had referred to in previous conversations with her friends, they were unable to confirm if this was the man's first name, surname, or perhaps even just a nickname. He was never traced. In any case, from interviews with Jean's friends and family, there was no evidence to suggest that Jean had any contact with 'Scotty' after 1945. It therefore seems unlikely that he was the 'Dr Scott' referred to in her note.

Interestingly, in a chilling comparison to the murder of Elizabeth Short (the Black Dahlia), who was of a similar age and appearance to Jean Spangler, both women were aspiring actresses who were known to have had abusive relationships with men in the military, both were brunettes, and both were known to have frequented the Florentine Gardens nightclub in Hollywood Boulevard, as had Mimi Boomhower. Jean had previously been a dancer at the Florentine Gardens and Elizabeth Short had lived close by. Both women living within five miles of each other.

So, with pressure mounting and still no concrete developments in the search for Jean Spangler, L.A.P.D. detectives re-questioned potential witnesses from the night of her disappearance. The last confirmed sighting of Jean had been from Lillian Marks, the eyewitness at the grocery stall in the Farmers Market. Lillian Marks remembered that Jean was apparently waiting for someone, between approximately 6pm and 6.30pm on the night of October 7th. A new appeal for information brought forward two further witnesses who believed they had observed Jean around 10pm on the night of her disappearance – more than three hours later than the previously last known sighting. Jean was spotted with a *'clean-cut, good-looking man'* close to the corner of Vine Street and Hollywood Boulevard, approximately 3.5 miles northwest of the Farmers Market. The pair were eating hot dogs and appeared to be smiling, seemingly in good spirits and in no apparent distress.

This appeared to be a significant development, proving that Jean was still alive and well, at least three hours after she had phoned her sister-in-law from the Farmers Market. The revelation opened up a series of new and intriguing possibilities for the investigators. Jean had left home on foot that evening, which seemed to indicate that someone must have picked her up from the market, as it was extremely improbable she would have walked more than three miles along the streets of L.A. alone at night to Griffith Park, at a time when rumours of a returning serial killer had heightened the city's sense of fear. Also, and perhaps crucially, this new sighting placed Jean less than three-quarters of a mile from the Fern Dell entrance to Griffith Park, the location at which her purse had been discovered. Wondering whether to initiate another search of the park, police pressed the witnesses to confirm the accuracy of their sighting. However, while both witnesses were certain that the lady they had seen was indeed Jean, they both now thought they may have been confused and had actually seen Jean on October 6th, the evening before her disappearance. It was a bitter blow for the detectives.

Part Three:

Nevertheless, despite this disappointment, another positive sighting of Jean followed. Three independent witnesses confirmed that they had noticed Jean at the Cheesebox Restaurant, a fashionable late-night eatery located at 8033 Sunset Strip (approximately three miles from the Fern Dell entrance to Griffith Park) between 1.30am and 2.30am in the early hours of October 8th, seven hours after the last-known confirmed sighting at the Farmers Market. All three witnesses positively identified Jean from photographs shown to them. Al 'The Sheik' Lazaar, a popular and well-known DJ on Sunset Strip, noticed Jean sat in a booth arguing with two men. As he approached their table to check if Jean was alright, he was impatiently waved away by one of the men.

Lazaar described the man as '*a clean-cut fellow about 30 or 35*'.

The proprietor of the restaurant, Terry Taylor, and a newsboy stood outside, also reported observing Jean with two men, one of whom they noted '*appeared clean-cut*'. The phrase '*clean-cut*', used by all the witnesses to describe one of the men, was a much more commonly used expression than it is today. Its original definition encompassed many things, including a young man who seemed conservative, respectable, trustworthy and reliable, in addition to being superficially neat, and well presented.

A busy Sunset Strip
in the 1940's

Even more crucially, later that same night, at a gas station, heading north on the Strip, a woman who closely resembled Jean called out for help. Around 3am a young man drove into the gas station in a blue-grey convertible. In the passenger seat was an attractive woman matching Jean's description. The gas station attendant, Art Rodgers, approached the car.

'Fill her up,' the young man said, *'we're heading to Fresno.'*

'Sure', replied the attendant.

After pumping the gas, Art Rodgers wiped the windshield and could not help noticing that, '*the beautiful girl in the passenger seat'* appeared ill at ease. The attendant thought that it seemed an extremely late hour to be undertaking such a journey. Fresno was more than 200 miles away, nestled deep in the San Joaquin Valley. He remarked on the distance, but the young man ignored his comment, thanked Rodgers for the gas, and sped away.

However, as they drove off, Rogers noticed that *'the woman shrank down in the passenger seat and cried out, "Have the police follow this car!"'* The attendant called the police immediately, but by the time a patrol car arrived, the convertible was long gone, and the officers were unable to locate it.

Interestingly, a number of illegal abortion rings were operating in Fresno at that time. One particular ring, a highly sophisticated and successful one, operated from an apparently legitimate florists. The florist's store was, in fact, a 'front' for the mob who offered an abortion service which included guaranteed secrecy, a privately chartered limousine, and even a flying service in which women were picked up by aeroplane from as far away as Los Angeles and San Francisco. There were often many ladies on these unscheduled flights, all being simultaneously transported for illicit terminations. The abortions were apparently performed at a secret location in the Manchester area of Fresno by a French doctor.

This mysterious doctor did not appear to have a licence to practice medicine in California. His service was an expensive one, costing $350 for the *'complete package'* (approximately $4,400 today). It seems the abortion business was just one of many illegal rackets being operated by the Fresno based mob at that time. However, the members of the Fresno underworld also enjoyed a high level of police protection, implying that many law enforcement officers were 'on the payroll' at that time. During an F.B.I. investigation, which took place in 1950, an anonymous lady who had paid for the abortion service reported that the gangsters had boasted to her of *'enjoying ironclad protection.'*

Although this seems hugely significant, there appears to have been little effort by the L.A.P.D to follow up this most meaningful of leads. The Police Department at that time was suspected of ties to the mob, which may explain the lacklustre nature of the investigation from some of the officers involved.

Although the crucial sighting of a lady resembling Jean at the gas station, coupled with the multiple witness accounts of Jean at the Cheesebox Restaurant, ultimately led the police to yet another dead end, the botched abortion theory seems a highly credible one in explaining the mysterious disappearance of Jean Spangler. However, other equally plausible theories would surface later.

And there, for the time being, the trail in the quest to solve Jean Spangler's disappearance went cold. Yet, as time marched on, several other sightings would emerge which cast doubt on whether Jean was actually murdered that night, instead suggesting that she may have been either abducted, or perhaps even staged her own disappearance.

A 13-year-old schoolgirl named Shirley Ann Morse, who had been Jean's neighbour on Colgate Ave and had often seen or spoken with her, told the police that she had seen Jean on Thursday October 13th, six days after the last previously confirmed positive sighting and five days after Jean's discarded purse had been uncovered in Griffith Park. Shirley Ann was riding to school on the school bus in North Hollywood when a large 1936 Black Packard sedan pulled up at the stop lights alongside the bus. Shirley Ann happened to look down at the car and (due to her higher viewing position from within the bus) had a clear view inside the car. She noticed Jean in the passenger seat. Unlike many of the other sightings, in which witnesses had only identified Jean from her photograph, Shirley Ann knew her well, and was 100% certain that the lady in the car was indeed Jean Spangler,

'I could see Jean plainly inside the car and I recognised her positively,' **Shirley Ann** later told detectives*, 'She was nervous and frightened looking. I am certain it was Jean. She was huddled in the right side of a black sedan driven by an older man.'*

A Black 1936 Packard Sedan

Despite the certainty of the witness, the police do not seem to have taken this sighting seriously, perhaps because of the schoolgirl's age. If Shirley Ann's statement was genuine, it does show that Jean was still alive almost a week after the discarded purse had come to light, which strongly suggests that the purse may have been a cunning decoy to send the police in the wrong direction.

Shirley Ann Morse's sighting of Jean seems to be corroborated by several other witnesses who all claimed to have seen Jean later that same morning (October 13th), and on the following day. They all described seeing Jean with *'an older man in an automobile.'* The same couple were spotted in Monterey, Salinas, and then Stockton, in Northern California. These sightings seem to suggest than Jean and the 'older man' were moving north, away from Los Angeles. However, there does not appear to have been any concerted effort to confirm these sightings as the police instead continued to concentrate on other lines of investigation, such as a gold earring which was discovered on South Ogden Ave, close to Jean's home. The earring was shown to Jean's sister-in-law; however, she was unable to positively confirm that it belonged to Jean.

As well as a possible link to the Fresno mob's abortion racket, the L.A.P.D. also suspected that Jean's disappearance may have been related to the Los Angeles underworld, with whom she was alleged to have had some contact. In her late teens and early twenties Jean had worked as a dancer at the Florentine Gardens, a nightclub owned by Mark Hansen and Nils Thor Granlund (both known to have ties to the mob). The Florentine Gardens was also frequented by well-known L.A. mobsters such as Anthony Cornero, Mickey Cohen, Davy Ogul and Frank Niccoli. The link might seem tenuous; however, Jean had reportedly been spotted just two weeks earlier with Davy Ogul, in Palm Springs and, then again, in Las Vegas with both Ogul and Frank Niccoli. Both men were under indictment for conspiracy at the time of Jean's disappearance and had both slipped away from police surveillance and subsequently been reported missing. Niccoli, a few days prior to Jean's last known sighting, and Ogul just two later, on October 9th. Perhaps they had fled California to avoid prosecution, taking Jean with them? The police certainly considered it as a working theory. Another, darker, possibility was that both Ogul and Niccoli had been killed by the mob, who may have been concerned that they might 'rat' to the authorities during police questioning. Detectives interrogated several known mob associates, including Thomas Ellery Evans and Mark Hansen (who had both already been questioned during the Mimi Boomhower investigation and over the murder of Elizabeth Short). However, they were unable to shed any further light on Jean's disappearance. Jean's sister, Betsy, also testified that neither she nor Jean *'had ever acquainted with Ogul, Cohen, or any of his associates.'* In addition, Jean's mother Florence, publicly stated that, *'Jean was not the kind of girl to get mixed up with people like that.'*

The police would have to wait several more weeks until a break finally came in the investigation. However, once again, it raised more questions than answers. Detectives received an anonymous tip-off informing them it would be *'in their interest to check a vineyard close to Cucamonga'* (a city located at the foothills of the San Gabriel Mountains, 40 miles east of Downtown Los Angeles). On inspecting the vineyard, officers discovered the body of Frank

Niccoli, tossed into a pit lined with quicklime. In a confusing twist, evidence uncovered at the scene seemed to indicate that Niccoli had been killed and buried sometime before the disappearance of Jean Spangler. Despite an intensive search at the vineyard, investigators could not locate the bodies of either Davy Ogul or Jean Spangler.

According to Jack Dragna, another L.A. mobster interrogated by the police, at the time of their initial disappearance Ogul and Niccoli had just been released from prison on a bail bond worth $75,000, fronted for them by Mickey Cohen. After the two men had chosen to abscond, Cohen had been forced to honour the outstanding bail bond (today's equivalent of almost $1 million) effectively putting him out of business. In a fit of anger, Jack Dragna claimed, Cohen had ordered the hit. However, to complicate matters further, Jack Dragna owned an incinerator in which victims of the mob were rumoured to have been cremated, removing all trace of their existence. Had Dragna, known as 'The Capone of L.A.', merely pointed the authorities in the wrong direction to deflect suspicion from himself?

The body of Davy Ogul was never recovered. There were no further confirmed sightings of him ever reported. It was generally assumed he had met the same fate as Frank Niccoli – and perhaps that of Jean Spangler.

Nevertheless, another possibility emerged a few months later, in spring 1950, when a customs agent working in El Paso, Texas, reported seeing Ogul with a woman who closely resembled Jean at a local hotel. A clerk working at the hotel also positively identified

Jean from a photograph shown to him. Despite this apparently important development, there were no entries in the hotel's register under the names 'Ogul' or 'Spangler' and no further witnesses could be found to corroborate the sighting. If the couple had been Davy Ogul and Jean Spangler, they had left the hotel and the El Paso area quickly.

Detectives, it seems, were still no closer to solving Jean's case. Despite an extensive search, both in El Paso and at the vineyard, no sign of Davy Ogul or Jean's bodies were unearthed.

And, with the mob connection theory proving to be yet another blind alley in the hunt for the missing dancer and actress, the investigation stalled. No new active leads were garnered and the L.A.P.D.'s Missing Persons Bureau issued a statement conceding that they had,

'We have received no further information, other than the numerous screwballs that have come in and tried to identify themselves with the case, but have added nothing to the fund of knowledge. One of these screwballs even had pictures of Jean in his billfold but he didn't even know the girl personally and was released.'

Exactly twenty days after Jean's disappearance temporary custody of Christine was awarded to Dexter Benner, despite a bitter court battle with Jean's mother, Florence.

Throughout 1950, and well into 1951, the messy court battle deepened. Benner accused Florence of trying to poison Christine's mind against his present wife, Lynn, by referring to her as *'not Christine's mom'* and that *'your proper mum will be home soon'*.

Benner's lawyer aggressively questioned Florence, demanding to know, *'Did your daughter ever have a henchman of Mickey Cohen as a sweetheart?'*

FAILED—Dexter Benner, former husband of the missing Jean Spangler, with his present wife Lynn and his daughter Christine, 6, as judge blocked effort by Mrs. Benner to adopt the child. Jean Spangler, television actress, disappeared Oct. 7, 1949.

Dexter Benner with his wife Lynn Lasky and Christine

Florence turned to the bench and replied, *'I only wish I knew, Judge Doyle.*

Jean's mother was also accused of giving her granddaughter a doll which she had named *'Jean'*, and *'to think of your mother every time she held the doll.'*

Florence denied this.

Benner repeatedly refused to allow Florence any visitation rights with her granddaughter, despite a court mandated order, and was eventually forced to serve fifteen days in jail for contempt of court. Following Benner's release he took Christine and fled the state. His disappearance became another temporary mystery (although he did resurface several years later).

Meanwhile Jean's mother continued publicising her daughter's disappearance, in a vain attempt to keep the story alive. Her mood fluctuated widely, one day convinced that Jean was still alive; the next, falling into deep despair, as this recently unearthed letter written several years later, to her daughter-in-law Sophie reveals,

'Sophie,
We still are doing all we can to find Jean, and that is always the paramount thing in my mind. All else is minor. I please urge you to try and recall details of events just prior to the time Jean dropped from sight. So many things have been bungled, that any new clue, any idea, might be instrumental in tracing her. I am hopeful that the Los Angeles police have some new clues.
Do you recall Jean ever saying she was "fed up" with show business and would like to get away? She once conceded that she regretted being plunged into the whirl of show business, but emphasised that it was a

momentary attitude. Jean actually was crazy about the life, I think. She liked the work and the attention it brought.

She worshiped the child. After all the trouble and the distasteful court battle she went through to gain custody, I know she wouldn't just walk off. It meant too much to her.

Yours, Florence'

For the next three years, on the anniversary of Jean's disappearance, the *L.A. Times* published an updated plea for information. A movie screenwriter and columnist Louella Parsons, and Jean's mother Florence, both offered rewards of $1,000 for information concerning Jean's disappearance or current location. However, despite the offer of a the reward receiving nationwide publicity, no further clues were forthcoming.

By late 1952 Florence's health had deteriorated rapidly and she seems to have relinquished any hope of seeing her daughter alive again, telling the *L.A. Times* that, *'I know that Jean would never have left willingly. She loved her home and her baby too much to ever do that. But, I just don't feel that she is alive anymore. Somehow, I have lost the feeling that she is alive . . .'*

The career of Captain Harry Didion did not seem to suffer unduly, despite the L.A.P.D.s failure to locate Jean. He would serve with distinction and was later given the crucial role of arranging security for the 1959 visit to the US of Russian Premier Khrushchev. A character in the long running TV police drama *Dragnet* was even named Harry Didion in his honour. After retirement he kept searching for Jean in his own time and at his own expense, but sadly to no avail.

Dexter Benner eventually resurfaced in Jacksonville, Florida, many years later. He lived a blameless life before passing away in May 2007 at the age of 87. He was survived by his wife of 58 years, Lynn, and by Christine, his daughter from his marriage to Jean. Now known as Christine Williams, Jean's daughter has since shunned the limelight and the intrusive glare of the media.

In more than 70 years since Jean's disappearance only two further theories have emerged that may explain the mystery. Both, however, are not proven and the authorities remain sceptical.

Firstly, it was speculated that Dexter Benner's second wife Lynn (to whom he had been married only four weeks at the time of Jean's disappearance) was formerly married to Ely Lasky, a well-known L.A. mobster closely connected to Mickey Cohen. Lynn had also been witnessed previously in the company of Dave Ogul. Did Lynn use her mob connections to arrange for a 'contract' to be taken out on Jean, thus simultaneously freeing her new husband of his maintenance payments to his ex-wife, and effectively granting him custody of his daughter. It must be remembered that Dexter Benner's only alibi for the day of Jean's disappearance was given by his wife. This alibi seems to have been taken at face value by the police and was not investigated. However, there seems to be little evidence to support this theory, other than an alleged family tie to the criminal underworld. Lynn Benner passed away in 2019, at the age of 94. During her lifetime she became an accomplished artist, exhibiting in both Florida and California. Following her death, and in compliance with her last request, her ashes were mixed with those of her husband Dexter, and their combined remains spread upon the waves of the Atlantic Ocean.

A slightly more compelling theory in the disappearance of Jean Spangler came in 2006, and from a surprising source. Retired L.A.P.D. detective Steve Hodel published a book, *Black Dahlia Avenger,* in which he makes a convincing claim that his own father, a doctor by the name of George Hodel, was responsible for a series of unsolved murders and disappearances in 1940s Los Angeles. In fact, it would later emerge that George Hodel had been interviewed by the police in 1947 as a suspect in the murder of Elizabeth Short. Was George Hodel possibly linked to disappearances of Mimi Boomhower (see *Erased* Chapter Four), and to that of Jean Spangler. There is no direct evidence connecting him to either case, however three points of interest do leap from the page. Firstly, George Hodel was known to frequent the same nightclubs in Downtown L.A. as Jean Spangler. Secondly, George Hodel was believed to be one of the L.A. surgeons performing illegal abortions at that time. Thirdly, and perhaps, most uncannily, he drove a 1936 Black Packard Sedan – identical to the vehicle in which Jean was witnessed by Shirley Ann Morse from the school bus, after a week after her disappearance.

In researching his father's past, Steve Hodel became convinced that his late father had committed the murders at the L.A. home in which the family had lived in at the time, and then disposed of the bodies nearby. Steve Hodel returned to the home in 2012 with a cadaver dog. Not only did the dog pick up the scent of human remains in several areas, including an alleyway behind the house, a soil sample taken from that same alleyway was privately tested by a forensic anthropologist, who confirmed that the sample *'came up positive for human remains.'*

Dr George Hodel

However, Steve Hodel has been denied access to the house, which is now a private home, and the L.A.P.D. has declined to investigate his claims further.

Was George Hodel the mysterious 'Dr Scott'? We may never know for sure. The serial killer theory remains now, as it did in 1949, yet another tantalising and unproven possibility in the quest for the truth about what really happened to the beautiful Jean Spangler.

Jean's father, Cecil, passed away in 1962 at the age of 67. Her mother, Florence, despite being broken by the mysterious disappearance of her daughter, lived to the age of 97, before finally passing away in 1991. Jean's elder sister Betsy passed away in 1996 at the age of 76 and her brother Richard in 2003 at the age of 85. They all left this earth still never knowing the fate of their sibling.

Was Jean murdered after a botched abortion? Did the L.A. mob really dispose of her body? Was she yet another victim of a still unknown serial killer? Or perhaps Jean and Davy Ogul double-crossed Frank Niccoli and escaped to Mexico? Or did she simply choose to abandon her daughter and begin a new and solitary secret life, far away from the limelight? Many people have speculated, dozens of articles have been written, and podcasts recorded.

However, the painful truth is that we are no closer now to solving the enigma surrounding Jean's disappearance than we were more than seventy years ago, on the night she smiled, winked, and waved goodbye to her daughter for the final time.

Scan here for extra photographs and digital versions of the images contained in this chapter

A Brief History of the
Black Dahlia

An Extensive Look at
Crime in 1940's LA

Interview with Jean's
sister-in-law, Sophie

Jean Spangler in the
Marx Brothers' short,
Mummies Dummies

The website of Steve
Hodel, Investigator

The 'Legs-on-the-Train' Murder

'No one cares about the man in the box, the man who disappears.'
Christopher Priest, *The Prestige* (1995)

Part One:

The usual chain of events in a missing person's story begins when friends or family realise a loved one is missing. Someone uncharacteristically misses an appointment, fails to arrive home from a night out, or leaves their house, apparently without a care in the world, only to never return. Ever.

The authorities are informed, an investigation begins, and the missing person's family begin their anxious vigil, as they wait for news with a thousand unanswered questions on their minds. Where are they? Will they be found? What happened? Why did they disappear? Occasionally, as in the previous stories in this series, the missing person never returns; leaving loved ones forever tormented by the enigma of their disappearance. Happily, more often than not, the missing person is found or returns home of their own free will. This chapter, however, details a far more unusual circumstance. What happens when the police discover a dead body, yet no one has been reported missing? Instead of one mystery, we are presented with two.

This is one such story.

London, February 1935.

Recovery from the Great Depression was proving to be a long and monotonous process for the typical working-class family in Britain. Some were lucky enough to be employed, others converged on the capital city, from the North, Wales, Scotland, and Ireland, all searching for work and creating a vast itinerant and anonymous labour force.

The winter had been bleak, and the news from Europe equally grim, as Adolf Hitler announced the re-armament of the German military. Londoners were grateful to be distracted from poverty and politics for a moment, as the city began its preparations for King George V's Silver Jubilee celebrations. However, on Monday 25th February 1935, a macabre discovery underneath the seat on a Southern Railways electric train at Waterloo Station, cast some unwelcome attention on the metropolis.

S.14617.   WATERLOO STATION.
VIEW OF GENERAL OFFICES & CONCOURSE FROM ESCALATOR.

The 2.03pm passenger train from Hounslow, via Twickenham, arrived at Waterloo Station on time. Following the departure of the passengers, the carriages and interior were due to be cleaned by railway employees prior to the train's onward journey on the loop route. Twenty-five minutes or so later, around 2.30pm, while cleaning one of the compartments, a Southern Railways employee by the name of James Albert Eves noticed a brown paper parcel, pushed well back under one of the seats in a third-class carriage compartment. There was only one passenger in the carriage at the time, who seemed to be waiting for the ongoing journey. He had apparently not noticed the seemingly innocuous package.

As was customary, Eves took the parcel to the station's Lost Property Office. However, while walking along the platform carrying the package, he noticed a curious suppleness at one end of the parcel.

'Have a look at this,' he said to John Cooper, one of his colleagues in the Parcels Office, *'It moves at one end. It feels like toes to me.'*

The two men examined the plain brown paper parcel, which had been tied both lengthways and across, with regular, household string. It was approximately twenty inches in length and nine inches in width. There seemed to be something suspicious about the anonymous package, and the two men decided to open it. Inside the outer covering of brown paper the parcel had been carefully packaged in two further layers of bloodstained newspaper. With trepidation they cautiously unwrapped the two layers of newspaper.

Contained inside was the lower part of two human legs, both severed from just below the knee.

The Railway Police were contacted who, in turn, contacted Scotland Yard's 'Flying Squad'.

C.I.D. officers, led by Chief Inspector Robert (Bob) Donaldson, and a divisional pathologist attended the crime scene. Several theories and rumours began to circulate among the police officers and railway station staff. Was it a hoax? Maybe the items were not real human legs after all. Or, assuming that they were, perhaps the whole thing was simply a perverse joke undertaken by a group of medical students?

However, a far darker possibility had already occurred to Chief Inspector Donaldson. Could the dismembered limbs be related to the unsolved Brighton Trunk Murders? The case had both fascinated and horrified the British public in recent months. During 1934 the bodies of two women had been discovered, dismembered and then stuffed inside large suitcases. The legs of one of the poor victims had been recovered from a suitcase at King's Cross Railway Station. The grisly similarity was already clear to everyone. Even before the Brighton Trunk Murders, the railways in Britain had already endured a reputation for similar crimes.

In 1924 a suitcase deposited by Patrick Mahon led to the discovery of the dismembered body of Emily Kaye, and in 1927 the murderer John Robinson left the body of his victim in a trunk at Charing Cross Station. No doubt, Chief Inspector Donaldson secretly feared that, a 'copycat' killer might be operating in the Capital.

GRIM DISCOVERY AT WATERLOO

New Dismemberment Mystery Faces Scotland Yard

MAN'S LEGS UNDER SEAT

THE GRIM DISCOVERY OF A PAIR OF HUMAN LEGS WRAPPED IN A BLOOD-STAINED PARCEL, WHICH HAD BEEN PUSHED UNDERNEATH THE SEAT OF AN ELECTRIC TRAIN, WAS MADE AT WATERLOO STATION, LONDON, YESTERDAY AFTERNOON.

The legs, which it has been established are those of a young man, were found by a carriage cleaner shortly after the arrival of a train from Hounslow via Twickenham.

They had been skilfully severed at the knee about 12 hours before, and rigor mortis had not set in. The feet were intact.

Meanwhile, an initial examination of the remains at Waterloo Station was made by the Divisional Police Surgeon. Firstly, it was instantly clear that the legs were real. Several other immediate observations were also made. The limbs had been wrapped in copies of different newspapers, a complete copy of the *Daily Express* from Friday 21st December 1934, and two sheets from the *News of the World*, dated Sunday 20th January 1935. Would this clue prove to be important? The information was passed to detectives.

At first glance, the dissection of the legs seemed to be fresh, and had not taken place more a few hours before their discovery. Rigor mortis had yet to set in. There did not appear to be any scarring, indication of disease, or infection on the limbs, thus ruling out a legitimate medical amputation.

Initially it was thought the legs might belong to a woman, as they were almost hairless and it appeared as if a form of hair removal cream, or white powder, may have been used. In addition, the victim's feet seemed to exhibit a very strange characteristic. Chief Inspector Donaldson decided it was now time to call in the country's leading pathologist and expert, Sir Bernard Spilsbury. In an era without television and social media, the exploits of men like Spilsbury, and the drama caused by a high-profile murder investigation, enthralled the public and provided a much-needed distraction from the humdrum of daily life.

Meanwhile, the investigators continued in their quest for the clues in the mystery of the 'Legs-on-the-Train' case (as it would soon be dubbed by the media).

Firstly, it was concluded, as the dismembering had taken place only recently, the victim may not yet have been reported missing. Their absence might not have even been noticed yet. That made a speedy identification of the person much harder. Secondly, where was the remainder of the body? A detailed search of the other carriages on the train was made, together with cloakrooms and parcel offices at other stations on the line between Hounslow and Waterloo. Fingerprinting was undertaken in the railway carriage and ticket collectors were questioned at every station along the line. Detectives were particularly interested in finding someone who might recall seeing a person carrying a brown paper parcel.

An assumption was made by investigators that the parcel was probably carried onto the train inside a suitcase. This would have been less noticeable, and far easier to then remove the package from the suitcase and slide it under the seat. The murderer could them simply exit the train with an empty suitcase, leaving the other passengers none the wiser. It was also conjectured that the use of a suitcase would help hide any blood that might drip from the package onto the floor of the train or over the clothes of the person carrying it.

In the meantime, Sir Bernard Spilsbury was instructed to conduct a thorough post-mortem on the two limbs and offer his findings to the police. His suppositions would prove most enlightening.

Spilsbury was able to conclude that the severed legs definitely belonged to the same person (a relief to the police, who at one point thought they might have been facing a double murder investigation). Still quite fresh in appearance, the amputations had apparently been carried out with great care, using a sharp knife or implement, and by someone with a least a small degree of medical knowledge or experience. There were no scars, marks of disease, or indications of infection on the legs which Sir Bernard Spilsbury concluded were those of a man, despite evidence of depilation and whitening. The separation of each limb had been achieved by a clean cut, directly through the soft tissues and across the joint, just below the level of the patella. Sir Bernard also noted that the legs were freckled and bore traces of light-coloured hair.

Perhaps most unusual, however, were the odd characteristics displayed by the victim's toes. The feet were pinched and the toes crushed together, with arched heels. This appeared to indicate someone who had become accustomed to wearing tight, or poorly fitting, footwear, or even women's high heels.

The police immediately considered *'a cross-dresser, a pervert, a homosexual, or a male dancer.'* In a less enlightened era, these assumptions were quickly made by detectives, who often presumed that the victim of this type of vicious and sordid murder must have somehow contributed to their own demise, perhaps by frequenting bars and nightclubs used by homosexuals or prostitutes. A search of nearby bars was conducted; but unfortunately, no new leads were forthcoming. The newspapers also indulged in some lurid speculation; however, the homosexuality theory was not considered suitable consumption for the average reader of the nation's daily newspapers, and that line of enquiry seems to have been very quickly dropped (by both the press and the police).

Spilsbury also concluded that the legs displayed good muscle development, perhaps indicating the man had been a manual labourer, dancer, or athlete. The muscles and the general condition of the bones also indicated that the limbs were those of a healthy, physically active individual, aged between twenty and fifty, but more likely between twenty and thirty years of age, Spilsbury thought. The absence of 'Harris Lines' also suggested that the man had not suffered from serious illness during his formative years.

The famous pathologist, using the length of the Tibia and Fibula bones, was able to calculate a man's height with a startling degree of accuracy. Using this formula, Spilsbury estimated that the victim would have been between 5ft 9in and 5ft 10in tall (with a possible margin for error of 1.5 inches), and of medium build, with size nine feet. Based on the light-coloured hairs on the legs, it could be safely assumed that the man had light hair and a pale complexion.

In contradiction to an earlier assumption, Spilsbury also now thought that, although the actual severing of the lower legs may have taken place only hours before their discovery, it was likely that death had occurred up to ten days earlier. This, of course, opened up the possibility that the victim may have been reported missing in the previous week or so. Missing persons files at all London police stations were checked again, this time for a period of ten days prior to the macabre discovery. However, no suitable matches were located.

The victim's limbs were then taken to Southwark Mortuary. The police also took the unusual step of employing two experts from London's Madam Tussaud's Waxworks, to prepare plaster casts of the deceased man's feet, in case an accurate representation might be needed at a later trial.

The earlier assumption, that the limbs had been left on the train in a medical student prank, was also dismissed by Sir Bernard Spilsbury. The unwashed condition of the feet and legs, and the lack of skin repair to the severed limbs, made it highly unlikely that death had occurred during a hospital operation or in a clinical environment.

Meanwhile, Chief Inspector Donaldson and Superintendent Helby had not been idle. Their enquiries had revealed that the train, on which the gruesome package had been found, ran a circular route which began and ended at Waterloo Station. However, during the course of the train's route, the carriages spent a short period of time waiting in a siding close to Hounslow station. The siding was bordered only by a low fence, making it comparatively easy for someone to access the track from the adjacent roadway. Detectives also noticed that the siding was not overlooked by houses at this particular location, giving almost unseen access to the carriages. Did the person dumping the parcel on the train also have some knowledge of the railway's timetable and routes?

This discovery also tied in with two further pieces of information gleaned from witnesses. The morning after the discovery of the legs, an employee of Southern Railways found some used bandages and cotton wool left on a carriage in the sidings at Hounslow. He had initially thrown them away, but after hearing the news, he retrieved the items and handed them to Mr A.J. Lawrence, the station master. In addition, the station master had already reported a sighting of three men acting suspiciously at the station during the previous afternoon,

'*I noticed them,*' he later explained to Chief Inspector Donaldson '*because of the strange way in which they were behaving. I thought they were Welsh miners. They were lounging about in the waiting room whispering to each other. One of them was particularly noticeable, because he had bright ginger hair.*

When the 1.06 train for Waterloo came in, the ginger haired man got inside, but the other two remained on the platform. I could not see whether the man who stepped into the train was carrying as parcel. As the train was leaving, the other two men shouted something to the man on the train.'

**Chief Inspector
Bob Donaldson**

The station master's sighting was confirmed by Harold Hillier, a clerk at the WH Smith Bookstall on the station platform, who also noticed the three men,

'They had a brown paper parcel about two feet long with them. They placed it on the platform until the 1.06 train for Waterloo came in. Only one of the men got into the train. He was about twenty-eight, medium height, and fair hair.'

At that time, many unemployed Welsh miners were being utilised by McAlpine Construction on various road improvement projects in the capital. The police thought that the sighting was a significant clue, however, after some investigation with the company, it was concluded that the labourers employed were essentially drifters, with no fixed address, and would be impossible to trace.

Examination of the railway timetable showed that the train had commenced its journey at 6.48am on the morning of 25th February. As none of railway's employees, or early morning cleaning staff, had noticed the package onboard the train at the beginning of the day, it could be safely assumed that the parcel had been placed on the train sometime between its first stop and its discovery at Waterloo at 2.03pm. A presumption was also made that the person involved had, in all likelihood, waited until the last possible minute before leaving the package and departing the train, to avoid being noticed and subjected to awkward questioning, before being able to leave the train. Therefore, it was highly likely that the offender had walked right past the ticket collectors at Waterloo Station not long after sliding the macabre parcel under the seat.

Working diligently, the police made enquiries at all twenty-two railways stations at which the train stopped that day. Unfortunately, other than the two potential sightings at Hounslow, their efforts were without success. The killer, or killers, had clearly covered their tracks well.

The Scotland Yard forensics team also carefully examined the single sheet of brown paper used to wrap the parcel.

The brown paper was of an ordinary and unremarkable type, apart from one small detail. In the bottom left-hand corner, in black crayon, had been written the figure '5', and on the opposite right hand corner appeared the number '14'. Although the police made a series of enquiries with newsagents, stationery suppliers, and post offices, they were unable to establish the relevance of the numbers '5' and '14'.

Meanwhile, detectives continued their efforts to uncover the identity of the missing person. The police even searched the parcels office at Brighton Railway Station, still working on the theory that the Brighton Trunk Murderer had struck again. Frustratingly for detectives the case seemed to pose more questions than answers, until a grim discovery was made on Tuesday 19th March 1935, by two boys playing on the bank of the Grand Junction Canal in Brentford.

Grand Junction Canal, Brentford

The two boys, Peter Emptage and Ronald Newman, were walking along the towpath towards Green Pond, watching a rat swimming in the water, when a large barge steamed past them. As it did so, something in its wake bubbled to the surface. The strange object appeared to be a sack with another item resting on the top. As the motion of the water pushed the object closer to the bank, the two boys, using sticks, were able to fish the sack towards them. As they did so, whatever had been resting on the top slipped off and fell back into the murky water. On cutting open the loosely tied sack, they discovered a headless and armless human torso. One of the boys, Peter Emptage, ran and told Frank Heath, a Great Western Railway employee, who in turn informed the police. He later described the discovery to a *Daily Mail* reporter,

'There were two small puncture wounds on the chest, like stabs. They were just about the region of the heart. There were several other stabs across the chest.'

The first policeman to inspect the torso thought that rigor mortis had yet to set in, indicating that death or amputation had probably occurred only a few hours before discovery (however, this would later be refuted). As darkness fell, the remains were left on the towpath, with two police constables maintaining an eerie overnight torchlight vigil. With the arrival of daylight the following morning, a pathologist's examination could be undertaken and a search of the canal bank started.

Sir Bernard Spilsbury carried out a full post-mortem on the remains almost immediately. They consisted of the upper part of a man's abdomen, which had been severed at the neck and at the elbows, leaving only the upper part of the arms. The torso was dressed in two items of man's clothing. A brown woollen vest, which was complete apart from a small portion around the buttonholes which had seemingly been cut away, and an unbuttoned grey flannel shirt.

There were ten cuts in the vest which corresponded exactly with the size and position of the ten stab wounds on the upper left chest of the torso, meaning the victim had been wearing the vest at the time of the stabbing. It was impossible to state conclusively if the wounds were inflicted before or after death. However, Sir Bernard thought that they were the most probable cause of death, although he was unable to confirm this.

When he cut open the torso, Spilsbury discovered that the chest had been severely crushed by a heavy object and that almost all the man's ribs had been fractured. However, he concluded that this had most likely occurred post-mortem, probably by a barge in the canal. He also concluded that the body had been in the water for some time, estimating that death had taken place around 15th February 1935 (a month earlier, and a few days before the discovery of the legs on the train). Based on the dimensions of the torso, he was able to provide a description of the man for Scotland Yard,

'Age 40-50, 5 feet 10 inches to six feet, fair hair, large freckles at the back of the neck up to the hairline, well built.'

The next task for the pathologist was to compare the torso found at Brentford with the legs recovered from Waterloo Station, and then determine if they came from the same body. If that was not the case, the police faced the chilling prospect of searching for a double murderer. Sir Bernard was joined as he made his gruesome comparison by Chief Constable Horwell, Superintendent Hambrook, and Chief Inspector Donaldson.

CANAL MYSTERY.—Searching a backwater of the Grand Junction Canal at Brentford yesterday, following the discovery of a male torso in the water.

Without the benefit of modern DNA analysis to aid him, Spilsbury was still able to conclude that both sections of the dismembered body showed similar muscular development, both had light coloured hair, identical freckles were found on the limbs and other parts of the torso, and that both parts appeared to be of a similar age. He was therefore able to determine that, in his opinion, there was a strong presumption that the severed legs and separated torso were indeed from the same body.

Spilsbury also noted another very significant feature. He stated that a degree of anatomical knowledge seemed to be present in some of the methods employed in the dismemberment, which was particularly striking in the removal of the lower arms, as elbow joints are particularly difficult to remove cleanly. However, other parts of the cutting where less professionally done. Perhaps the removal of the head had been a last-minute decision, he concluded, or conceivably more than one person had helped to carve up the body.

The removal of the lower arms was thought to have been done to make identification more difficult. The most likely reason for this, investigators believed, was that the victim had a distinguishing tattoo, or fingerprints which might already be in police files.

Meanwhile, detectives continued their painstaking enquiries. One intriguing possibility presented itself. Just three hundred yards along the waterway from the location in which the torso had been recovered, the canal is crossed by the Southern railway bridge which carries the line from Hounslow to Waterloo. Four-hundred yards along the canal in the opposite direction is the District Line railway bridge on the route between Hounslow to Acton. A system of locks situated on the canal at this point also caused the water to run at an appreciable speed, meaning a body dumped in the canal might easily move three or four hundred yards. The torso had been discovered only three miles from the point at which the train containing the severed legs had commenced its journey, Hounslow Station. Brentford Station was also close by and was the second point at which the train stopped on its journey towards Waterloo Station. Detectives pondered a chilling possibility; that the murderer had boarded the train at

Hounslow with the sections of the body in two packages, then alighted at Brentford with the torso, leaving the severed legs under an empty compartment seat (which would then be recovered by the cleaner at Waterloo Station later that same day).

A second scenario was also considered. Had the sack containing the torso been thrown into the canal from the same train, as it passed over the canal bridge? It was a strong possibility. Chief Inspector Donaldson ordered several tests to be carried out to test the theory. Officers carrying similarly weighted sacks, travelled on trains as they passed over the canal bridges. Four sacks were heaved through carriage windows by detectives as it crossed over the bridges, travelling in both directions. However, on each occasion the sacks, no matter how dexterously thrown, landed well clear of the canal. One sack in fact landing eighteen yards clear. Coupled with the speed of the train at this point, the narrow width of the waterway, and the difficulty in forcing the sacks through a train compartment window, it now seemed highly unlikely that the sack had been thrown from a passing train. In addition, anyone witnessed carrying a sack onto a train might have appeared extremely conspicuous. Detectives concluded that the killer probably living close by, or at least had sufficient knowledge of the local area to know a convenient location at which to dispose of the body; and one which could not be easily overlooked. This seemed more probable than the two other alternatives, either someone trying to force a package through a train compartment window, or a person having walking a considerable distance towards the canal, carrying such a suspicious and unwieldy parcel, without being witnessed by a single person.

The sack that had contained the torso, together with the victim's clothing, were sent away for further examination at the Police Laboratory, in an attempt to yield a maker's name. The vest was stained, but it could not be determined if these marks were merely as a result of its prolonged time in the canal. Although the items had been profoundly damaged from their exposure to water, the vest still bore a faded tab bearing the manufacturer's label - Messrs. Harrott and Company Limited, 50 Rose Street, Aberdeen.

Chief Inspector Donaldson contacted the company, who stated that the vest was one of their most popular styles, which retailed for two shillings and six pence. Many thousands had been distributed for sale via their London and Provincial wholesalers, and it would be impossible to track down a single item. The manufacturers thought the only reason which might account for one portion of the vest having been cut away around the buttonholes, was that it carried a laundry mark which might have potentially led to the identification of the owner. Other than that, the clothing failed to yield any further clues.

The sack which had contained the dismembered torso was also examined. It was found to be both quite old and well used, although it still bore a distinguishable company name and logo:

W.W. OGILVIE, Flour Factors of Flour Mills, Montreal, Canada.

It was discovered that Ogilvie's retained a London sales agent, and that the sack had been manufactured in Canada around 1929. Unfortunately, the sack was one of a large number (probably one among tens of thousands) that had been exported from Canada to the UK, and as such was identical to any other. Yet another dead end for the investigating officers.

Part Two:

A substantial effort was made to drag the canal, in the search for the mysterious object which the two boys said had fallen from the sack as they pulled it in towards the bank. Chief Inspector Donaldson thought it may have been the victim's head, which could have potentially made identification much easier. A team of officers, working with the River Police, dragged the canal as far as the Great Western Dock – the point where the Grand Union Canal meets the Thames – and upriver for three miles as far as Richmond, but without a positive result.

Every locks, sluice gates, induction pipes, towpaths, and bridge that crossed the canal were searched, but no new clues were forthcoming.

Superintendent Horwell even considered draining an entire stretch of the canal, but this was deemed impractical and financially unachievable. Whatever potentially vital clue fell to the silty bottom of the canal that day would sadly remain a mystery.

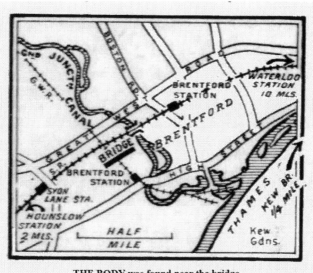

THE BODY was found near the bridge indicated on map

On Monday 25th March, almost a week after the discovery of the torso, a potential break in the case finally presented itself. A road-sweeper working in Isleworth, less than a mile from the canal, found some articles of men's clothing, stuffed inside an old, discarded cistern on a piece of waste ground behind Quaker Lane. The lane was a lonely thoroughfare running from London Road, in Isleworth, to the Great West Road, and on the edge of a new housing estate. A forensic examination of the clothing was ordered and the items were duly noted and bagged into evidence as follows:

'Worn, but still serviceable:
(1) A Khaki undercoat, with large pockets, of the type commonly worn by labourers;
(2) A white shirt with black stripes;

(3) A grey overcoat, badly torn;
(4) A cap;
(5) A fawn mackintosh'
There was no underclothing among the articles.'

Scotland Yard had publicly voiced the opinion that *'the murdered man must have been of the wandering labourer type and employed on contracting work, moving from job to job, and had then been involved in a brawl.'* Therefore, the discovery of some working man's apparel stuffed inside an old cistern did fit that theory, particularly as nobody had reported anyone - even vaguely matching the police's description - missing.

Meanwhile, on the same day, a lockkeeper, who was walking towards The Fox Inn reported witnessing a stationary motor-car in Hanwell, at the southern end of Green Lane close to the Grand Union canal. The lockkeeper was able to provide a description of the vehicle, noting that it carried a north country registration number. He thought it suspicious, and told the police, *'The road is a dead end, very close to the canal, and is never normally used by vehicles, unless people are dumping rubbish in the water.'*

In an even more sinister development, a dagger was recovered from the canal by a police motorboat, in the water near Hanwell. However, it yielded little information and couldn't be positively linked to the torso. Meanwhile, a woman also contacted the police convinced that she had seen a human head in the canal a week or so earlier. As a consequence, Thames River Police dragged another section of the canal between the Hanwell locks and the junction with the River Brent, however, this also failed to unearth any new evidence. Nonetheless, this did convince the police that the area of Hanwell was crucial and search efforts were intensified there.

Another gruesome discovery soon followed, two miles away from the canal. A refuge worker at the council rubbish tip in Ealing uncovered a human skull. The skull, which was located in one of many dust gathering machines at the facility, had a severely damaged parietal bone and seemed to be covered in acid splashes. The macabre item was taken to Southwark Mortuary to be examined by Sir Bernard Spilsbury. However, the skull did not provide the hoped for breakthrough on the case. The pathologist concluded that the skull was clearly a discarded medical specimen, and was so old it crumbled when touched. Once again, the investigation appeared to have stalled.

The apparent discovery of a human head in the canal on 26th March created huge speculation and excitement in the case. Unfortunately, the 'head' turned out to be part of a tailor's waxwork dummy, thrown into the water as a hoax!

Detective's attention returned, once again, to the brown paper and newspapers in which the severed legs had been wrapped. Investigators noticed that a small section from one of the sheets of newspaper had been cut away. Had it been removed to hide a vital clue, officers wondered? Perhaps a house number to aid a paperboy, or a membership number for a participant in a gift book scheme run by the newspaper. Enquiries were then made with the Fleet Street offices of the newspaper who confirmed that the missing portion of the page did correspond exactly with the part of the page used to print customer's gift book scheme numbers on. Detectives were able to obtain the names and addresses of several hundred previous participants in the gift book scheme, all within a four-mile radius of the canal at Brentford, almost all of whom were traced and interviewed, but no useful information was forthcoming.

However, the brown paper used to wrap the severed legs yielded perhaps the most important piece of evidence yet; which brought detectives tantalisingly close to discover the identity of both the victim and the killer.

Forensic and photographic tests on the brown paper revealed that the words 'Hanwell Mental Hospital' had been previously written on there, and subsequenty erased. Chillingly, the Grand Junction Canal passed close by the grounds of the mental hospital. Two other words had also been written on the brown paper, and then erased, 'Ward' and 'Harry'. Had the victim been a patient at the hospital, or perhaps the killer had been an employee or a patient there? Scotland Yard officers made enquiries at the hospital which yielded two vital clues. Firstly, the hospital had wards numbered '5' and '14' (which corresponded with the numbers written on the corners of the brown paper) and, secondly, an employee at the hospital recognised the writing as his own and suggested that the brown paper had, in all probability, been originally used to wrap a parcel send to someone in either Ward 5 or Ward 14. It was a staggering breakthrough.

Now convinced that the key to the mystery lay in the Hanwell area, a new appeal for witnesses brought forward a fifteen-year-old schoolboy who provided another vital clue.

Alfred Holliday, of Church Walk, Brentford, gave the following statement,

'About four weeks ago I went to the canal bank from the bridge on the Great West Road, to try and find a torch I'd lost. It was nearly dusk when I reached the canal. I was walking along the tow path, just by the railway bridge at Brentford. I was looking for my torch in an old empty house, which is in a field beside the canal path. Suddenly I saw a man in some bushes besides the canal. He was about 5 feet 9 inches, and I noticed that he was wearing a light mackintosh. He was very broad and had a slouch hat pulled down over his eyes. Beside him the man had a strange looking tin chest or trunk. He looked towards the road in the opposite direction.

I was scared, so I ducked back, and without finding my torch, made my way from the spot. I don't think the man saw me.

When I was about five yards away, I heard a series of splashes in the canal, as though the man had thrown in a number of objects. I hurried away, as I did not like the look of the man, and I said nothing about it until I read of the finding of the torso. Then a picture of this man immediately leapt into my mind.'

Had fifteen-year-old Alfred seen the killer? It certainly seems likely.

Although the Hanwell lead appeared to be a positive one, it ultimately led nowhere. A further search of the section of canal by Brentford Locks was ordered, and all bargees that operated on the Grand Junction Canal between Coventry and London were interviewed, but still no further information could be gleaned.

Another public appeal for information followed, which led to a huge number of responses from the public. However, the police later issued a statement saying, *'That nothing of any useful character has been found as a result of these new enquiries.'*

Male missing persons files from police constabularies across the entire country were scoured, in the hope that any new missing persons reports might shed some light on the baffling case, but still no matching descriptions were found.

Meanwhile, Chief Inspector Donaldson made another concerted effort to link the discovery of the body parts with the 1934 Brighton Trunk Murders, but no concrete connection could be established (other than the similar means of disposal). Every railway company in mainland Britain assisted by searching all cloakrooms, waiting rooms, and parcels offices, at every railway station in the country, but the victim's lower arms, upper legs, and head were never recovered. However, it was noted that in the first Brighton Trunk murder case, the capital letters 'FORD', which had formed part of a longer word, had been found on the torn sheet of brown wrapping paper which had been used to wrap that victim's torso. Several police officers wondered if this meant that the victim of the first Brighton murder had a connection to

'BRENT-FORD'. The similarities in the cases were certainly striking. Nevertheless, no provable connection was ever established.

An official inquest finally opened in Southwark on 10th May, headed by the Coroner for South London, Mr A. Douglas Cowburn. An earlier inquest had been postponed allowing more time for further police enquires. Although the mutilated legs had been first discovered more than two months previously, with little new evidence forthcoming, a further adjournment was granted until 6th June.

At the reconvened inquest Sir Bernard Spilsbury gave evidence, watched by more than fifty medical students in the gallery, who had all come to see the world-famous pathologist testifying.

First to give evidence, however, was James Eves, the cleaner who had originally discovered the brown paper parcel at Waterloo Station.

'The only person in the compartment', he stated, 'was a working man, about 5 feet 8 inches in height, wearing dark clothes, and probably in his forties. The man appeared to have just got into the train, which was about to return to Twickenham. I do not think he had any connection with the parcel.

The brown paper was crumpled, as if it had been used before.'

Sir Bernard Spilsbury was able to add a few more morsels of information to his original post-mortem findings,

'I found three detached hairs, four inches long – those of a woman, apparently – lying on the man's chest. These definitely were not the hairs of a man.' He also added that, *'In both the torso and the legs, there is practically a complete absence of blood. The stomach had been removed from the torso.'*

Sir Bernard also concluded that there was *'strong presumptive evidence to suggest that the legs and torso were from the same person'*, and he repeated his assertion that the murderer possessed *'some amount of anatomical knowledge.'*

The coroner then summed up the case for the jury,

'If Sir Bernard is right, certain facts stand out which seem to indicate that some person or persons had very good reason to conceal the identity of this individual. If the forearms had been tattooed, would their removal destroy a clue which might possibly lead to identification? Was the stomach removed to hide the cause of death and the vest left on the torso because there was no time to hide it?'

Chief Inspector Donaldson reported to the coroner that, *'In having regard to the definite statement of the pathologist to the effect that anatomical knowledge had been displayed, we are of the opinion that the murder could not been carried out either at a mortuary, public hospital, institution, or a medical school, without that person being detected. We are also of the opinion that the vest which the man had been wearing, if it was part of his usual clothing, was not one that would have been issued by any public body or hospital, and that the condition of his feet, which had not been washed in several days, were not in the sort of condition that a hospital patient's feet would have been in.'*

The coroner concluded there was not sufficient material to justify extending the case any further, nor enough evidence to definitely state a cause of death. An open verdict was recorded, although Mr Douglas Cowburn did point out that there was, *'more than a suspicion that this person met his death by foul means.'*

File notes written by the Scotland Yard detectives after the inquest, also detailed a point not released to the press. Sir Bernard Spilsbury had found clotted blood in the hair of the victim's armpit, which he stated, *'In my opinion suggested death from wounding, most probably from an injury to the cranium, and that if my deductions are correct, that there could then be little doubt that this is indeed a case of murder.'*

Chief Inspector Donaldson also believed that whoever had been responsible for this brutal killing had panicked, as there was undoubtedly a considerable risk in publicly and openly leaving the limbs on the train. In addition, he expressed some surprise in the ability of the killer to dispose of the forearms, head, lower portion of the trunk, and upper parts of the legs without detection, or without leaving a single clue behind.

So, the 'Legs-on-the-Train' Murder or, as it also became known, the 'Torso-in-the-Canal Horror', still remains an unsolved cold case, leaving several vital questions unanswered. Who was the killer? What was his connection to Hanwell Mental Hospital? Was a woman involved? Exactly where did the gruesome dismemberment take place? What was the motive? Was the killing connected to the unsolved Brighton Trunk Murders, or not?

The answers to all these questions sadly remain a mystery. Most poignantly of all is the other unanswered conundrum – Who was this brutally murdered man, and why did no one report him missing? Sadly, he seems to have been a missing person that nobody missed at all.

Chief Inspector Donaldson continued to periodically comb newly filed missing persons reports, however, no suitable matches ever came to light. Bob Donaldson was later promoted to Superintendent and, in 1945, was commended for his distinguished service, before retiring from the Metropolitan Police Force.

The darkest secret behind this story undoubtedly lurked somewhere behind the walls of Hanwell Mental Hospital, and is unlikely now to ever be revealed. Hanwell Hospital now forms part of the headquarters for the West London Mental Health NHS Trust; and in more recent years been used as a filming location for, among others, BBC TV's *Porridge*, ITV's *The Professionals*, and the 1989 Hollywood movie *Batman* starring Jack Nicholson.

Sir Bernard Spilsbury, aged 58 at the time of this case and at the height of his powers, was an intimidating and influential presence in court. After helping Britain's war effort as part of Operation Mincemeat in 1944, he took his own life in 1947 at the age of 70, following a number of personal tragedies. The medical journal *The Lancet* called him *'The greatest pathologist of the age.'*

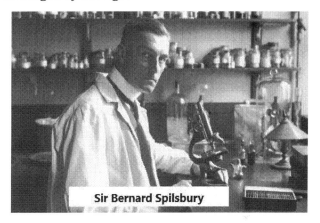

Sir Bernard Spilsbury

The dismembered parts of the unidentified victim were reunited and buried in a single grave at Streatham Park Cemetery on Tuesday 11th June 1935. The gravestone carries the simple epitaph,

'The Remains of an unknown Man.'

His story, his secret, and the name of his murderer are buried with him.

Scan here for extra photographs and digital versions of the images contained in this chapter

A Glimpse at 1930's
London

Grand Union Canal

More on the Brighton
Trunk Murders

Sir Bernard Spilsbury

'So tomorrow we disappear into the unknown'
Sir Arthur Conan Doyle, *The Lost World*

Part One:

Early on the morning of Monday 20th April 1925, an intrepid British adventurer and explorer set out into the uncharted jungles of Brazil's interior. Leaving from Cuiabá, the gateway to the wetlands of the Northern Pantanal, the journey that followed would not only lead to an enduring mystery, it would also inspire a Hollywood film franchise, not to mention at least two other movie characters and books. Together with his eldest son, Jack, and Jack's best friend Raleigh Rimmel, Percy Fawcett intended to journey deep into the heart of the hot, humid, impenetrable, and little-explored Brazilian jungle.

Accompanied by two native guides, Percy Fawcett hoped to discover somewhere deep in the jungles of Matto Grosso, the fabled lost city of 'Z', abandoned generations ago by an advanced and ancient culture. The riddle of exactly what happened on that expedition would become an enduring legend. Percy Fawcett, whose previous adventures had already motivated Sir Arthur Conan Doyle to create *The Lost World* in 1912, would go on to provide the inspiration behind the fictional movie character made famous by Harrison Ford. In fact, the character of Percy Fawcett even appears in the 1991 novelisation *Indiana Jones and the Seven Veils*.

During my research for this story, I unearthed many texts and articles all claiming to have pieced together the clues behind one of history's enduring riddles. In particular, one rarely seen document caught my eye, a seventy-two-year-old article by Brazilian journalist and investigator Edmar Morel. In it, Morel claimed to have at last uncovered the truth behind the mysterious 1925 disappearance of Lieutenant-Colonel Percy Harrison Fawcett, British army officer, war hero, cartographer, explorer, archaeologist.

In addition to being the inspiration behind the fictional movie hero Indiana Jones it seems Percy Fawcett was many other things. This is his story.

Fawcett was born in August 1867 - the age of the great Victorian explorers and adventurers - at his parents' home, Villa Devonia, in the quiet English seaside resort of Torquay. Raised in an eccentric family, perhaps he was always destined for adventure and a touch of wanderlust. Percy's father, Edward Boyd Fawcett, was Indian born and an army officer, English cricketer, and Fellow of the Royal Geographical Society, who also managed to spend his way through two family fortunes. Percy's brother, Edward Douglas, was an experienced mountain climber and an Eastern occultist. Their passions would help shape Percy's destiny, which in turn indirectly led to many of the adventures featured in the Indiana Jones' movies.

Percy followed in his father's footsteps and enrolled at the Royal Military Academy in Woolwich, London, where, in 1886, he was commissioned as a lieutenant of the Royal Artillery. After meeting his future wife, he joined the 1st Cornwall Artillery Volunteers and was promoted to captain, before later serving in Hong Kong, Malta, and Ceylon (now Sri Lanka). Much like Indiana Jones' father in *Indiana Jones and the Last Crusade* (played by Sean Connery), Percy Fawcett became fascinated by his father's passion for archaeology and adventure and joined the Royal Geographical Society (RGS) in 1901. This gave him ample opportunity to study surveying, mapmaking, South American exploration, and archaeology. It is no coincidence that the *Raiders of the Lost Ark* opens with Indiana Jones deep in the South American jungle.

Just like the movie franchise, the government utilised Percy Fawcett's unique skills to fight against the enemies of the time. Indiana Jones fought the Nazis in Egypt, while Percy Fawcett also served in North Africa for the British Secret Service. Later, he also worked for the War Office on Spike Island in County Cork, Ireland.

On 2nd May 1906 Fawcett was rewarded by the Royal Geographical Society with his first expedition to South America, to assist in the mapping of a remote jungle area on the frontier between Brazil and Bolivia. Now thirty-nine years of age (coincidentally the same age as Harrison Ford when he first appeared in *Raiders of the Lost Ark*), it was here that Fawcett began his lifelong obsession with uncovering the hidden secrets of the Amazon. After arriving at La Paz in Bolivia in 1907, his party journeyed into the dense interior where Fawcett claimed to have encountered a sixty-two-foot-long anaconda snake, so terrifying that he was forced to shot it. He reported the incident to the RGS and, although scientists ridiculed his claim, he unsurprisingly developed ophidiophobia – a fear of snakes. Although, at the time, Western European explorers had never encountered snakes of that size, there have been many sightings in more recent years of anacondas and pythons measuring at least twenty feet in length. The anaconda emerges from water and is tightly coiled, which may have perhaps made it difficult for Fawcett to estimate its true size, although the description he gave in his journals seems to be in no doubt. His letters and diary entries were later collated and published by his son, Brian, under the title *Exploration Fawcett* and provide a lens through which modern day readers can observe how early twentieth century explorers viewed the uncharted territories of South America, and which used language and attitudes prevalent at that time,

'We were drifting easily along in the sluggish current not far below the confluence of the Rio Negro when, almost under the bow of the boat, there appeared a triangular head and several feet of undulating body. It was a giant anaconda. I sprang for my rifle as the creature began to make its way up the bank, and hardly

waiting to aim, smashed a .44 soft-nosed bullet into its spine, ten feet below the wicked head. At once there was a flurry of foam, and several heavy thumps against the boat's keel, shaking us as though we had run on a snag.

With great difficulty I persuaded the Indian crew to turn in shore-wards. They were so frightened that the whites showed all round their popping eyes, and in the moment of firing I had heard their terrified voices begging me not to shoot, lest the monster destroy the boat and kill everyone on board, for not only do these creatures attack boats when injured, but also there is great danger from their mates.

We stepped ashore and approached the reptile with caution. It was out of action, but shivers ran up and down its body like puffs of wind on a mountain tarn. As far as it was possible to measure, a length of 45 feet lay out of the water, and 17 feet in it, making a total length of 62 feet. Its body was not thick for such a colossal length - not more than 12 inches in diameter -but it had probably been long without food. I tried to cut a piece out of the skin, but the beast was by no means dead and the sudden upheavals rather scared us. A penetrating foetid odour emanated from the snake, probably its breath, which is believed to have a stupefying effect, first attracting and later paralysing its prey. Everything about this snake was repulsive.

Such large specimens as this may not be common, but the trails in the swamps reach a width of six feet and support the statements of Indians and rubber pickers that the anaconda sometimes reaches an incredible size, altogether dwarfing the one shot by me.

The Brazilian Boundary Commission told me of one killed in the Rio Paraguay exceeding 80 feet in length!'

Fawcett also reported encounters with other mysterious animals not known to zoologists at that time, including the giant – and highly poisonous – Apazauca spider (the Goliath Birdeater), a small, black dog-like cat, called the Mitia, the Manguruyú (a gilded catfish), the Minhocão (a giant earthworm, which measured up to eighty-feet in length, and is now believed to be extinct), and a strange dog with a double nose, which was dubbed the Maricoxi. The latter may well have been the double-nosed Andean Tiger Hound, an extremely rare breed of dog originally found in Bolivia. The animal's distinctive nose is split into two completely separate nostrils.

On his return to England Percy Fawcett became close friends with Sir Arthur Conan Doyle; both men had developed an interest in spiritualism and the occult. Fawcett's Amazonian experiences would provide the inspiration behind Conan Doyle's 1912 science-fiction novel *The Lost World*, with Fawcett partly providing the inspiration for the story's protagonists Professor Challenger and Lord John Roxton. In later years, George Lucas would later use these characters as templates for the creation of Indiana Jones.

Bitten by the bug of adventure, Fawcett returned to South America for seven further expeditions between 1906 and 1924 (having retired from the army in 1911 at the age of forty-four). Like a sponge, he soaked up native folklore and the ancient tales of exploration left behind by the *conquistadors*.

During his treks, Fawcett's encounters with the local, indigenous tribes and villages were mostly amicable; largely as a result of his courteous behaviour and generous gift giving. However, during these trips he also undertook serious academic research into the possible existence of a number of lost cities, located deep in the uncharted Matto Grosso region of Brazil (now commonly spelt Mato). Fawcett developed several theories regarding the location of these forgotten civilizations. One day, buried deep in the archive vaults of the cavernous National Library of Rio de Janeiro, Fawcett unearthed a yellowing old parchment known as Manuscript 512, which had been initially rediscovered in 1839, by a man named Manuel Ferreira Lagos. The document was believed to have been originally written in 1753 by João da Silva Guimarães, a Portuguese slavetrader and explorer (who belonged to a group known as the *bandeirantes*, or 'Soldiers of Fortune'). The manuscript, which had been partly eaten by worms, was headed *'A Historical Account of a Large, Hidden, and Very Ancient City, Without Inhabitants, Discovered in the Year 1753.'*

Guimarães described how, *'after a very long and troublesome peregrination, incited by the insatiable greed of gold,'* his party had ascended a steep mountain path until they discovered the ruins of an ancient city laid out below them. There, *'at the foot of the jagged mountain'*, hidden from civilization, the party discovered huge stone arches, a statue, wide roads, and a temple containing intricate hieroglyphics - *'The ruins well showed the size and grandeur which must have been there, and how populous and opulent it had been in the age when it flourished.'*

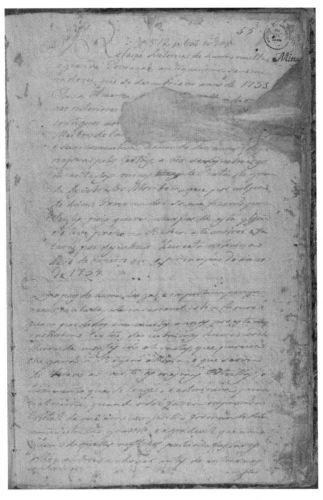

Although the manuscript had been written following a well-documented series of Portuguese expeditions into the *sertão* (hinterland) of the state of Bahia, no details of the lost city's exact location were forthcoming. It seems that the *bandeirantes* were primarily in search of a number of fabled gold and silver mines located there; and clearly had little intention of revealing the city's whereabouts to anyone else.

While the veracity of the ten-page manuscript is by no means certain, it was rumoured that the original Portuguese explorers had unearthed a number of ancient gold coins. This convinced Fawcett, and several other late nineteenth and earlier twentieth century explorers, that the existence of an advanced Pre-Columbian civilization somewhere in the uncharted interior was genuine.

Fawcett's interest in the civilization described in Manuscript 512 convinced him that the document referred to the mythical lost city he named 'Z'. Nevertheless, according to the one-hundred-and-fifty-year-old manuscript, rather than explore their discovery immediately, the *bandeirantes* had decided to return to civilization and organise a larger expedition, armed with suitable equipment to exploit their discovery. They sent a record of their findings back to the city with one of their guides, an indigenous tribesman. However, although the native runner returned to the city with their handwritten log, the explorers were never heard of again. With their disappearance, the location of the mythical city Fawcett believed to be 'Z' was lost forever.

By 1914, Percy Fawcett's certainty in the existence of 'Z' was absolute. He had researched many Amazonian dialects and invested significant amounts of time immersing himself in the ancient folklore of the native tribes. During his earlier excursions deep into the Rain Forest, Fawcett had already discovered shards of intricately decorated ancient pottery along the mouth of the Amazon River, and noticed puzzling, raised mounds of earth, which he thought might contain valuable secrets that would lead him to 'Z'.

He began to plan and map out an expedition in search of the fabled kingdom he excitedly referred to a 'Z'. Never a fortune hunter, Fawcett was a fearless archaeologist and cartographer and a recipient of the Royal Geographical Society's Gold Medal. Much like his fictional counterpart, Indiana Jones, Fawcett was also not afraid to venture into uncharted territories, armed with little more than a knife, a compass, his Stetson hat, and a strong sense of purpose. Yet, he was aware of the risks – and had already encountered many of them personally. Fawcett had been ambushed by hostile tribesmen, with poison darts fired from blowpipes, many of whom had never seen a white man before; and had managed to emerge with maps of regions from which no previous expedition had ever returned. Fawcett himself had referred to the Amazon basin as *'the last great blank space in the world to be mapped and explored.'*

However, his plans were interrupted by the outbreak of the Great War in 1914. Despite being forty-seven years of age, with thinning grey hair, Fawcett volunteered for duty and was posted to Flanders to command an artillery brigade. By March 1918 he had been promoted to Lieutenant-Colonel, been mentioned in dispatches three times by Field Marshall Haig and awarded the Distinguished Service Order.

Yet, the horrors of the Great War appalled him and, following the armistice, he soon yearned for a return to South America and yet another chance to uncover 'Z', the city he believed was the cradle of a lost civilization. In 1920, Fawcett embarked on a solo expedition that ended abruptly at a place he named Dead Horse Camp. Unfortunately, delirious with fever, Fawcett shot his ailing pack animal and withdrew from the jungle in defeat. Tantalisingly, before illness had forced him to abandon his expedition and return to civilization, Fawcett believed he had just unearthed the remains of an outpost belonging to the lost city. Although having lost fifty-three pounds in weight, he recorded in his journal that he felt *'none the worse for it.'*

Nevertheless, he was determined to return. By 1924, now aged fifty-seven, nearly destitute, and dismissed by many as a crackpot, it seemed that he would not be able to secure sufficient financial backing in England for what would surely be his final attempt to find the mythical 'Z'. In a letter to the RGS, he wrote angrily, *'It is of course bound to come out eventually that a modern Columbus was turned down in England.'*

He recorded in his journal that, *'The last few years have been the most wretched and disillusioning in my whole life, full of anxieties, uncertainties, financial stringency, underhand dealing and outright treachery. My wife and children have been sacrificed for it, and denied many of the benefits they would have enjoyed had I remained in the ordinary walks of life.'*

Finally, however, Fawcett's anger and determination were rewarded. By the beginning of 1925 he had received sufficient financial backing from the RGS in England, from various news organisations (in return for regularly filed dispatches), from the American

Geographical Society, and the Museum of the American Indian.

In order to lessen the amount of equipment needed, Fawcett was determined to travel light. The party would consist of just Fawcett himself, his son Jack, and Jack's best friend Raleigh Rimmel. Only two native Bakairi guides were hired, each one especially chosen by Fawcett for their fitness, good health and loyalty to each other. Fawcett firmly believed that the smaller his search party, the less opportunity that news of his quest would reach either native tribes (who may be hostile to outsiders), or other European explorers intent on beating him to the location of the mythical kingdom.

The small team of five equipped themselves at Cuiabá in Matto Grosso, before heading into the wilderness complete with eight mules, two horses, a pair of dogs, a selection of canned foods, powdered milk, a.22 revolver, flares, a sextant, a chronometer, and a secret antique map. Fawcett left strict instructions, stating that if the expedition failed to return, no rescue attempt should be made. He did not wish any rescuers to suffer the same fate.

They departed from Cuiabá on Monday 20th April 1925 and headed quickly northward across the dry forest region known as the cerrado. Although fifty-seven, Fawcett was fighting fit, his steely blue eyes and strong physique giving him the appearance of a movie star (something he fully intended to become if his mission was successful). It is perhaps fitting then, that the story based on Fawcett's legendary quest would inspire a famous movie sequence of its own, the iconic opening scene in Raiders of the Lost Ark.

The first few days of their trek into the interior were comparatively trouble-free; the terrain they encountered consisting mostly of small, twisting trees and open savanna grassland. A few ranchers and gold prospectors had already established settlements there, and established pathways through the forests which eased their progress. On day one, the party covered seven miles from Cuiabá; on day two, a further ten.

Fawcett was feeling strong, fit, and motivated. He often pushed far ahead of the rest, in such of clues, cutting his way through the undergrowth using a specially designed eighteen-inch-long machete.

In the early days of their quest, Fawcett was able to send the native guides back to civilization with notes and letters he had written. As well as personal letters to his wife, there were updates for newspaper editors (which formed part of his financing agreement), and a progress report to the President of the RGS, the Earl of Ronaldshay. At a meeting of the RGS in London, on Monday 16th June 1925, the Earl was able to report to the RGS members that,

'Colonel Fawcett is at the head of a small mobile expedition, making its way from west to east at right angles, to the series of rivers which flow from south to north into the main stream of the Amazon. Colonel Fawcett makes no secret of his belief that there still exists, hidden in the dim recesses of the vast tropical forests, evidence in buildings certainly, and in people possibly, of the great Inca Empire.'

Meanwhile, the newspaper editors, who gratefully received Fawcett's communiques, were less interested in the dry facts of the explorer's quest, and more so in the sensational headlines it enabled them to publish,

'Fawcett's notes relayed to civilization by Indian runners over a long and perilous route.'

'Three Men Face Cannibals in Relic Quest.'

'The Grim Region – From Which They May Not Return!'

However, as the men ventured further into the interior, communication with the outside world became harder. To add another obstacle to their quest, the weather became unbearably hot and humid. During the day, not even the shade of the Buruti palms could provide any relief. Even at night, the temperatures did not seem to drop, and thick, swirling clouds of mosquitos swarmed above their campsite. In one dispatch Fawcett wrote that the *'fish in the Cuiabá River were literally cooked alive.'* At night the men were forced to wrap themselves in netting to prevent the risk of mosquito bites and infections, with only tea and biscuits on which to survive.

On the fifth or sixth day, as the group approached the Manso River, approximately forty miles north of Cuiabá, yet another obstacle presented itself. The entire area was infested with huge, voracious ticks, and Raleigh Rimmel was bitten badly on the foot by one of the tenacious creatures. The bite became infected and swelled rapidly, forcing him to remove his shoes. He was unable to walk properly and could only ride on horseback, although at each jolt, the pain shot through him. In order to help Raleigh recuperate, Fawcett decided to rest for a few days at a cattle-breeding ranch on the edge of the frontier. The large redbrick ranch was owned by Hermenegildo Galvão, one of the most powerful and ruthless ranchers in the Matto Grosso basin. So remote was the ranch's location that Brazilian law was considered irrelevant and unenforceable there. Galvão even employed a mercenary posse of hired gunmen to patrol his vast estate and kill any native tribesman who threatened him or trespassed on his land.

According to a later report by Galvão, and sounding uncannily like a scene from an Indiana Jones movies; one night, during their stay at the ranch, Fawcett produced a strange object wrapped in cloth, from among his belongings. He carefully unwrapped it and showed it to his host. The object was a ten-inch-high black basalt carved idol, with almond-shaped eyes and intricate hieroglyphics carved on its chest. The novelist, and good friend of Fawcett's, H. Rider Haggard had previously given the statuette to him, as a good luck charm, convinced it was a relic from the lost city of 'Z'. According to legend, the idol sent a small electric shock up the arm of anyone susceptible to its unknown forces.

Part Two:

After a week of rest and recuperation the party of five left the safety of the ranch and headed eastward towards Bakairí Post, a garrison set up by the Brazilian government five years earlier. The outpost was referred to by the settlers as '*the last point of civilization*', although even the journey there was anything but civilised. The trail became ever harder, as Fawcett, Jack, and Raleigh hacked their way through dense forest, jungle, steep muddy gorges, mountainous hillsides, and treacherous, rocky rivers, with their roaring rapids, overhanging trees, and cavernous waterfalls. Even simply wading across these perilous rivers and streams presented further dangers to the party. Before crossing any expanse of water everyone was forced to check for the presence of scratches or cuts anywhere about their person. Even the slightest trace of blood might attract shoals of deadly piranhas. Another imminent water-borne danger came from the deadly eel-like fish known as the candiru. Fawcett had encountered the candiru on an earlier expedition and noted in his journal,

'The candiru seeks to enter the natural orifices of the body, whether human or animal, and once inside cannot be extracted.'

Having previously witnessed the agonising spectacle of a candiru being removed from a man's penis, Fawcett added, '*Many deaths result from this fish, and the agony it can cause is excruciating.'*

After a month of arduous trekking, they finally crossed Bananalzhino and reached Bakairí Post, which in 1925 was a settlement of no more than twenty huts: each one rather resembling the upturned hull of a boat and tightly woven from thatch and wood. The Brazilian government had attempted to 'acculturate' the Bakairí tribe, and Fawcett was horrified by what he witnessed. In a letter to one of his financial backers in New York, he wrote,

'I am appalled by the Brazilian methods of civilising the Indian tribes. The Bakairís have been dying out ever since they became civilised. There are only about 150 of them left. They have in part been brought here to plant rice and manioc ... which is then sent to Cuiabá, where it fetches, at present, high prices. The Bakairís are not paid, are raggedly clothed, mainly in khaki govt. uniforms, and there is a general squalor and lack of hygiene which is making the whole of them sick.'

At Bakairí Post, Jack and Raleigh encountered other, even more remote, native tribesmen from the Xingu region, whom they described as *'wild'* and *'absolutely naked, carrying seven-foot-long bows with six-foot arrows.'*

By Tuesday 19th May 1925 (Jack's twenty-second birthday) the party made their final preparations to head north from Bakairí Post, beyond the thick forests and a range of imposing mountains, into what they described as *'absolutely unexplored country.'*

It was only now that their journey became unimaginably more difficult. There were now no discernible paths or tracks. And although, somewhere above, the sun was beating down, no light could penetrate the carpet of thick trees that towered 150-feet above them. Huge creepers entangled their legs, and their bodies sweated profusely in the oppressive heat. Above their heads, swarms of stinging insects, known as piums, attacked any bare flesh, leaving their arms and necks like pincushions. Vampire bats, anaconda snakes, and venomous scorpions posed a constant threat. The three English explorers grew ever wearier, and their native guides displayed an unnerving and open fear of the potential threat from the nearby unfriendly Xingu tribes, with their deadly poisonous spears.

After nine more arduous days the party reached a sight on the Rio Batovi, that Fawcett had dubbed Dead Horse Camp, the place at which he had shot his pack horse on his previous expedition five years earlier. The bones from the animal's skeleton still lay there. The three explorers were now almost exhausted. Fawcett recorded, in his final despatch to reach civilization, that,

'We were attacked by the wickedest fly on earth, almost invisible, biting like a mosquito, and very active. We covered ourselves in nets, but the bugs slipped through them.'

By this stage the two native Bakairi guides had become so nervous, frightened by the threat from the many hostile tribes of the Upper Xingu, that Fawcett decided to send them back with his final series of dispatches and letters. He informed the two guides that he would attempt some further communication with the outside world at a later stage, but that it was unlikely anyone would hear from them for at least a year, perhaps two. In reality, Fawcett had always intended to send the guides back. He did not want anyone, not even his wife, to know the exact route or location of the lost city.

Meanwhile, Raleigh's infected foot had remained ulcerous and swollen, with very little skin left on it. Fawcett tried to persuade him to return to Cuiabá with the guides, but he refused, saying he would not leave his friend, Jack.

So, on the 29th May, the native guides left carrying the last dispatches and letters the outside world would ever receive from Lt-Col. Percy Fawcett. In one of his final messages, Fawcett noted,

'By the time this dispatch is printed, we shall have long since disappeared into the unknown.'

The guides also brought Fawcett's final letter to his anxious and long-suffering wife, Nina, with them:

'Nina,

Here we are at Dead Horse Camp, latitude 11 degrees 43' South and longitude 54 degrees 35' West, the spot where my horse died in 1920. You need have no fear of any failure.'

Yet, in his final report to the North American Newspaper Alliance Fawcett noted his coordinates as 13°43'S 54°35'W. His discrepancy in the latitude might have been merely a typographical error. However, he may have intentionally concealed his actual location to prevent anyone else from using his notes to find the lost city.

Fawcett, Jack, and Raleigh waved goodbye to their trusted guides and set off, carrying their equipment on their backs, deep into the interior. This time they were on foot, the forest was now too dense for horses or mules.

The world would not notice their absence for almost two years . . . .

Finally, in January 1927, having received no further communications from Fawcett and his party, the RGS together with the British government wired a request to the Brazilian government, hoping for some information. After making several enquiries the Brazilian authorities reported back,

'No sign has been found of the colonel's whereabouts or evidence of his fate. It must be assumed that Fawcett and his companions have perished.'

This might well have been the end of the story. After all, any attempt to locate the missing men would almost certainly fail (as Fawcett had warned). Yet, from the outset, rumours began to surface which, far from solving the mystery, only served to deepen it. Had Fawcett been slain by native tribesmen? Was he being held captive? Had he become a white god of the Indians? Had he renounced civilization in favour of a life in the jungle?

Nina Fawcett also refused for many years to acknowledge that her husband had died. Like Percy, she believed in spiritualism and occasionally reported telepathic communication with her husband, through various intermediaries, in which he told her he was alive and well.

Soon after the RGS's public declaration that Fawcett had perished, there was an outpouring of volunteers offering to help locate the lost explorer. Several men tried and failed; one lone searcher died in the attempt. Most assumed that hostile natives had killed the men, as several tribes were known to be nearby at the time, including the Kalapalos (thought to have been the last tribe to have seen them), the Arumás, the Suyás, and the Xavantes - whose territory in the Xingu they were last thought to be entering. Many privately believed that a party of just three was too small to survive in the jungle, and that Fawcett's expectation that all the indigenous tribes would be friendly was probably naive.

However, fellow explorer Henry Costin, who had accompanied Fawcett on several previous expeditions, expressed his doubt that Fawcett would have perished at the hands of native tribesmen. Costin believed that Fawcett typically enjoyed good relations with them; and was more likely to have succumbed to either exhaustion, infection, or lack of food. Perhaps there was still some hope?

The first tangible and credible clue came from a French hunter, in late 1927. He claimed to have been shooting alligators near the city of Cuiabá when he came upon a bearded white man he thought to be aged about sixty (Fawcett would have been sixty in 1927). The two men exchanged some remarks in English and the French hunter departed. This encounter caused a flurry of speculation. Was the bearded man really Percy Fawcett?

In 1928 Commander George Miller Dyott led an official expedition to trace Fawcett. He was an American born British explorer, aviator, and adventurer, who had served as a squadron commander for the Royal Naval Air Service during the Great War. Dyott advertised in the London newspapers for volunteers to accompany him. Among the 20,000 applications he received, one came from Roger Rimmel, the elder brother of Raleigh.

The day after his wedding to Persis Wright in New York, Dyott and his new bride sailed to Brazil for their honeymoon. Dyott then promptly left his wife at the hotel and set off in search of Fawcett. He managed to trace Fawcett to a remote native village called Nahukwá, where the first solid piece of evidence was uncovered among the low roofed huts. The son of the village chief Aloique had a necklace around his neck, on which was a small brass plate. The plate bore the name of the London firm 'W.S. Silver and Company', who had supplied Fawcett with some equipment in 1924. Fawcett had undoubtedly been in the village.

The tribesmen told Dyott that Fawcett and his two white companions had reached a river known as the Rio Kuluene in 1925. However, by that stage both Jack and Raleigh were exhausted, and the three men had rested there. From this point by the river, Fawcett led the group eastward. For five days and nights, from their vantage point on the hillside, the tribesmen told George Dyott that they could clearly see the smoke from the three men's campfires as they hacked their way through the jungle. On the sixth day there was no smoke.

The tribesmen were convinced that Fawcett and his companions had been massacred by the hostile Suyás Indians. Dyott forged on, nevertheless, hoping to reach the exact spot where Fawcett had been killed and find some definite evidence of his demise. Dyott was convinced that some arrow-like 'Y' shaped marks he had uncovered, carved into the bark of trees, were a map of some kind left by Fawcett. Shortly after this discovery, however, Dyott ran short of food and he dumped most of his equipment, fearing that Aloique, chief of the Anukukua tribe, was about to massacre his party (as Dyott had not brought enough gifts with which to bribe the native tribe). He barely managed to escape with his life, and he returned to civilization empty handed and exhausted.

Ultimately Dyott's expedition was discredited when it transpired that the brass plate worn by the chief's son had in fact been left behind by Fawcett on his previous journey into the region in June 1920. Undaunted, nevertheless, Dyott later published a book about his adventures, *Manhunting in the Jungle,* in 1930. He also co-wrote and starred in a 1933 Hollywood film based on his story, entitled *Savage Gold.*

Meanwhile, Nina Fawcett refused to accept the findings of Dyott's quest for her husband, saying,

'I still believe they are alive, but detained, and cannot get away.'

With no obvious solution, the mystery continued to persist well into the next decade.

From 1930 to 1931 the wonderfully named Canadian adventuress Aloha Wanderwell used a seaplane to search for Percy Fawcett. Still only twenty-four years old in 1930, Aloha was a colourful and controversial figure. She had already learned to fly a German 'Junkers' seaplane, and had clocked up more than 380,000 miles, across eighty countries, becoming the first woman to circumnavigate the globe in a 1918 Model T Ford. Aloha married the controversial figure Walter Wanderwell in 1925 (although she took to using his surname long before that – much to the chagrin of his first wife, to whom he was still married at the time). Walter Wanderwell had previously been jailed during the Great War on suspicion of being a German secret agent. At the time of their wedding he had also been under threat of arrest from the FBI under the *Mann Act* (a law that prohibited transporting women across state lines for immoral purposes).

Aloha and Walter Wanderwell, together with a small team, set off in May 1930. The Wanderwells set up camp at the Descalvados Ranch, outside Cuiabá, and began their quest for the lost explorer in a previously uncharted region of Matto Grosso. After several fruitless search attempts, scanning the ground below from their seaplane, they ran out of fuel on the Paraguay River and were forced to crash land (much like plane sequences in both *Raiders of the Lost Ark* and *Indiana Jones and the Temple of Doom*). They received help from the Bororo people, with whom they stayed for six weeks. Although they were able to film the first moving footage of the Bororo tribe to be seen by the outside world, they returned empty handed from their quest.

Twelve months after returning to the US, Walter Wanderwell was murdered in California. Although a member of his South American expedition crew was suspected at the time, the murder remains unsolved. Aloha never returned to Brazil to attempt a further search for Fawcett.

There were no further developments in the search for Fawcett until 16th October 1931, when a Swiss fur trapper named Stephan Rattin suddenly appeared at the British consulate in San Paulo, with a remarkable tale. Rattin spoke to the British consul-general, Arthur Abbott, who had known Fawcett personally. In a sworn statement, Rattin claimed to have been hunting near the Tapajós River, in the northwest reaches of Matto Grosso, when he found an elderly white man held captive in a native village. The man, who was clothed in animal skins, spoke to Rattin while the natives were distracted.

'Are you a friend?' the man asked Rattin.

'Yes,' Rattin answered.

'I am an English colonel,' he said, *'Go to the British consulate and tell Major Paget that I am being held captive.'*

According to the Swiss trapper, the old man had shown him a signet ring which closely matched the description of one Nina Fawcett had given to her husband. Rattin told the officials at the British consulate that he was prepared to lead an expedition back to the village to rescue the British colonel. Rattin's party of three trekked through the remote jungle for weeks, finally arriving at the Arinos River, where they constructed canoes from bark. In his final despatch, dated 24th May 1932, Rattin wrote that the expedition was about to enter hostile territory. The three men were never heard from again.

In November 1931, the Penn Museum in Philadelphia organised its own expedition to Matto Grosso. Although it had originally intended to make a documentary about the region, rather than search for the lost explorer, the expedition soon becoming embroiled in the mystery surrounding Percy Fawcett's disappearance.

While looking for suitable documentary material Vincenzo Petrullo, a well-known anthropologist and archaeologist, headed north from the expedition's base camp. After crossing the Kuluene River by canoe, he encountered Aloique, chief of the Anukukua tribe, who remembered seeing Fawcett six years earlier. Petrullo would later tell his story to *The Philadelphia Record,*

'I realized I had been following his (Fawcett's) *trail when I reached the village of the Kalapalos on the Kuluene river, a tributary of the Xingu. Two of the natives came to tell me of the visit and departure of three white men a number of years ago. That having been only the second time outsiders had come into their country, the incident was clearly remembered.*

They told how the white men arrived at Kalapalo village in the company of some Anahukua Indians who had guided them from their village on the Kuluseu, a march of four days. The white men carried packs and arms, but no presents for the Indians such as I had. The Kalapalu gave them food, biiju, and fish, and in the morning, having failed to dissuade the leader, the older man, from his project, they ferried the three men across the Kuluene River...It was explained to the Indians that by going east a wide river would be reached where large canoes could be found which would take the party home. The younger men were ill and were suffering from Borachudo sores (from the bite of the Black Fly), *and apparently were reluctant to go any farther. Subsequently for five days the Kalapalu saw the smoke of the travellers [as they lit a campfire each night]. It is presumed that on the sixth day they reached the forest to the east, for the smoke was not seen any more. Later a party of the Kalapalo found traces of the camps made, but not the white men.'*

Vincenzo Petrullo presumed that Fawcett had probably, *'died of thirst, or hunger, or disease somewhere in the dense forests to the east of the Kuluene River...I believe it would be impossible for Colonel Fawcett to be alive in that region without anyone knowing it. News travels fast there. Especially news concerning white men, because there are so few of them.'*

Petrullo was asked for his opinion regarding Stephan Rattin's apparent encounter with Fawcett a month before his own sighting.

'Ridiculous,' he explained, *'Rattin's sighting took place hundreds of miles away. And then there is the story of the animal skins. No one wears animal skins in that region. You would die from the stench if not from the heat. The Indians go absolutely naked.'*

The threat from indigenous tribes was not imagined nor exaggerated by explorers, however. Five American missionaries on a peaceful quest were slaughtered by tribesmen in 1945. Meanwhile, despite the dangers, rumours persisted that still enticed others to search for answers. Stories that a white child had been seen among some native villagers also fuelled speculation that Jack Fawcett had fathered a child with a native girl.

The quest continued for several years, with many risking their lives to locate Fawcett, including Peter Fleming, brother of James Bond creator Ian Fleming. In 1933, an official Brazilian expedition found Fawcett's compass in the jungle and later returned it to his family.

Meanwhile, Nina Fawcett maintained a steadfast conviction that her husband and son would one day reappear. Even twenty-five years later, in 1950, she told a journalist that she still, *'would not be surprised to see Percy and Jack walk through the door, Percy now aged eighty-two, and Jack forty-seven.'*

However, in 1951, seemingly irrefutable evidence of Fawcett's demise appeared to have been uncovered. Orlando Villas-Bôas, a Brazilian activist for the rights of indigenous peoples, was given the skeletal remains of Fawcett by the Kalapalo natives.

The tribesmen claimed that Fawcett had been murdered because he had slapped a young Kalapalo boy, and because he had not brought any gifts for the villagers with him.

Villas-Bôas had the bones analysed scientifically. The analysis apparently confirmed the bones were Fawcett's, however, Percy Fawcett's son Brian refused to accept this and demanded that the bones be examined in Britain by the Royal Anthropological Institute, who later released a statement stating that:

'The upper jaw provides the clearest possible evidence that these human remains were not those of Colonel Fawcett, whose spare upper denture is fortunately available for comparison. . . . Colonel Fawcett is stated to have been six feet, one and a half inches tall. The height of the man whose remains have been brought to England is estimated at about five feet, seven inches.

The bones were returned to South America and are apparently still in the possession of the Villas-Bôas family.

This announcement gave renewed vigour to Brian Fawcett's efforts to locate his father. In 1951, four years after the bones had surfaced, Brian Fawcett conducted his own quest for his father and the mythical city of 'Z'. He hired a small propeller plane and dropped more than 5,000 leaflets over the Mato Grosso jungle. The leaflets simply requested the following:

'Are you Jack Fawcett? If your answer is yes, then make this sign holding your arms above your head....

*Can you control the Indians if we land?.... Is P.H.
Fawcett still alive?'*

When he failed to receive any positive responses, he
undertook an aerial search for any physical signs of
'Z'. However, after many days crisscrossing the
Amazon, studying the landscape through powerful
binoculars, he began to fear that the legendary lost
city may never have existed at all.

Part Three:

In 1979 Fawcett's signet ring was located in a pawn
shop, fuelling speculation that the three men had been
killed by bandits, their valuables stolen, and their
bodies dumped in a river.

Even by the dawn of twenty-first century, with all our
modern technology and equipment, the mystery to
solve the disappearance of Percy Fawcett remains an
enigma. Modern expeditions utilising GPS, satellite
imagery, computer mapping, offroad vehicles, and
even television sets as gifts for the native tribes, have
still failed to unearth any definite proof of either Percy
Fawcett or the lost city of 'Z'.

The mystery still seems as impenetrable as the jungle
in which its secrets are held. However, during my
research for this story, instead of assuming that modern
technology might yet solve the problem, I took my
inspiration from *Indiana Jones and the Last Crusade*,
and returned to an older source of information, the
written word. Just as Indy studiously poured over the
journal of his father (Dr Henry Jones, played by Sean

Connery), I spent many hours searching historical archives looking for an account that might shed some more light on Fawcett's unexplained disappearance. Eventually my patience was rewarded by the discovery of this 1951 memoir from respected Brazilian journalist and researcher Edmar Morel. Morel's 1943 expedition, although previously reported, has been largely forgotten – perhaps due to the Second World War. Nevertheless, it seems to confirm many of the rumours surrounding the mysterious disappearance. This is Morel's original and unaltered record of his 1943

adventures, as it first appeared in 1951:

'I MEET A WHITE INDIAN AND SOLVE THE MYSTERY OF COL. FAWCETT

From two missionaries in the heart of the Brazilian jungle I heard the story that was to lead me to a solution of the Fawcett mystery. I came upon these two men of God, after weeks of perilous hunting for traces of Col. Percy Fawcett, the famous British explorer, his son Jack, and their companion Raleigh Rimmel.

My task was to determine the fate of these daring explorers who, twenty-six years ago, disappeared in the trackless forests of South America. And now, in the jungle mission house of Emilio Halverson and Thomas Young, I was given the vital clue that I lacked. It was a faded photograph of a native woman holding a white baby in her arms.

"I saw the baby first," Halverson said, "when I was travelling by dug-out canoe to the Indian villages on one of my journeys to spread the Gospel. Many canoes passed me on the way, but there was one that especially attracted my attention. In it was this Indian woman nursing a pure white baby. I took it as a curiosity."

He passed me the photograph while Halverson's fellow missionary, Thomas Young, took up the tale.

"In the years that followed we sometimes heard the natives speak of their white Indian, But I only saw him once. That one view of him, however, was enough to make me realise why the tribesmen said he was the son of Col. Fawcett's son. Although his hair was dark, he has a white skin and European features. His name is Dulipe."

"Then he is alive?" I asked the calm old missionary with growing excitement.

"Yes," he said.

At once I said I must go to him, but Halverson warned me against it. Dulipe belonged to the Kalapolas Indians – and they were notorious killers. But his warning only spurred me on. For if indeed the Kalapalos were such cruel savages, it might well be that they had murdered Col. Fawcett, Rimmel and Jack Fawcett twenty years previously – even though a woman of their tribe had given birth to Jack Fawcett's son.

The next morning, in spite of the forebodings of the missionaries, I set out with my search party accompanied by an Indian interpreter. We paddled upriver to the village of the Kuricuro. There, the Indians professed to know nothing of Dulipe or indeed of any other white men ever having been among them. But after much talk they allowed us to summon all the Indians for miles around to a parley.

Soon they began to appear, the Nafuquas, the Meinacos, the Autis, the Auras, the Kuricuros, and last of all the terrible Kalapalos, to whom Jack Fawcett's son Dulipe belonged.

But Dulipe had not come. Nor had Izarari, their chief. I made liberal gifts to the Kalapalos delegates who were present and asked them to take me to Dulipe and Izarari. Doubtfully, they agreed. A secret rendezvous was made and in a native canoe I was paddled to the prearranged spot. There, at last, squatting in the bows of a crude boat, I saw a young man, entirely naked – and white. Behind him, on the bank, arms folded, stood a native.

We hurried towards them. The native turned. It was, my guide told me, Izarari himself. I handed him gifts and through the interpreter began to question him. With a thrill of astonishment I heard Izarari speak openly and freely about the white man whose very existence had been denied by every savage we had so far met.

It was an opportunity I dared not miss. From my canoe I hastily unloaded the recording apparatus I had brought with me and then invited Izarari to continue. And I was able to record, for all time, what was surely the strangest interview any journalist has ever had.

Here is some of it, exactly as my recording machine took it down. It tells the story of the completion of my investigation:-

Morel: Where did white men die?
Izarari: They die in jungle.
Morel: Did they die of sickness or were they killed?
Izarari: They die by arrows.
Morel: Did Kalapalos kill them? (Izarari lowers his head. There is a pause)
Morel: Why did you kill white men?
Izaari: White men want to take Kalapalos into country of Caiapos Indians. Kalapalos not like to go into country of other Indians. White men start to push Kalapalos . . . .
Morel: So you killed them. Where did this happen?
Izarari: Four days' journey from here. White men die and Kalapalos come back.
I produced the pictures of Percy and Jack Fawcett and asked: "Were these the white men who were killed?" Izarari nodded and the mystery of Colonel Percy Fawcett was solved.

I confess that my excitement at bringing my mission of investigation to a successful close prevented me, for a moment, from savouring the full horror of Izarari's confession. My first impulse, when I did so, was to take steps to see that the killers – above all, Izarari himself – should be brought to book. But I soon realised that was impossible. Izarari's savages would only butcher my whole search party if we attempted any arrests.

So I continued to pretend friendship for Izarari so that at least he would give me permission to speak to Jack Fawcett's son, Dulipe. He did so, and, again, through the interpreter, I had a hasty conversation with the white Indian who knew nothing of civilization save the fact of his own descent from white men.

Then I had to leave. I could not take the responsibility of allowing my party to remain longer with these dangerous savages. Back through the jungle we canoed and trekked for weeks – impatient to tell the world of our discovery.
EDMAR MOREL, 1943'

When Edmar Morel returned from the Amazon interior, his story was not believed. In fact, some claimed that he had faked both the recordings and the photographs he took. For a brief moment in 1951, the expedition by Orlando Villas-Bôas and the discovery of (what was thought to be) Percy Fawcett's bones, vindicated Edmar Morel. Even after the skeletal remains were identified as not belonging to Fawcett, Morel's claims were not diminished, since they did not rely on the bones as proof or justification. Furthermore, there seems to be no reason for Izarari to have fabricated such a story, since he did not gain financially from it. In fact, he merely ran the risk of reprisals from the Brazilian authorities. In addition, the evidence of the white child, Dulipe, although not definite, is nevertheless compelling.

By the time Morel published his full account in 1951, Izarari had passed away, probably taking with him the only absolute confirmation of what really happened to the British explorer.

However, just like the Indiana Jones movies, the story of Percy Fawcett continues to spawn sequels.

During the 1960s, the Danish explorer Arne Falk-Rønne journeyed to the Mato Grosso. He would later write that he had learned of Fawcett's fate from a third party, who in turn claimed to have overheard the story directly from one of Fawcett's murderers. Seemingly, Fawcett's party had capsized on the river and lost most of the gifts intended for the native tribes. Continuing without gifts was a serious breach of protocol, which angered the Kalapalos tribe, resulting in the men's deaths. The bodies of Jack Fawcett and Raleigh Rimmel were then thrown into the river. Being an older man, and therefore more revered in Kalapalo culture, Percy Fawcett received a proper burial.

A Russian documentary film crew ventured into the Brazilian interior in 2003, primarily in search of the lost city, and concluded that Fawcett's 'Z' may have in fact been the legendary El Dorado, the lost city of the Incas, an advanced civilization from the other side of the Andes. They also concluded that Fawcett had most likely met his end at the hand of the Kalapalos Indians.

New York writer David Grann visited the tribe in 2005 and was surprised to learn that the Kalapalos preserved a vivid oral history about Fawcett, who was remembered among the tribe as being among the first white man to visit them. Their oral tradition seemed to agree with the earlier version told to George Dyott; relaying the same story describing how Fawcett, Jack, and Raleigh had headed eastward. The Kalapalos then warned Fawcett that if they continued in that direction they would be killed by *'fierce Indians'*, who occupied that territory. Fawcett, however, was determined and insisted on continuing. The Kalapalos told David

Grann that they observed smoke from the Fawcett's campfires each evening for five days, before it disappeared on the sixth.

Grann's findings were later detailed in his 2009 book *The Lost City of Z,* which also became a movie in 2016.

The quest to discover the lost city of the Incas, seems to have obsessed western explorers almost since the discovery of the Americas. The evidence points to Percy Fawcett becoming yet another in the long line of adventurers to have succumbed to this fascination.

In 2017, John Hemming, an historian and leading expert on the Incas and the indigenous Amazon tribes, wrote an article in *The Spectator* magazine, in which he spoke about *The Lost City of Z,*

"The Lost City of Z is a very long way from a true story – and I should know".

According to Hemming, many years after Fawcett's disappearance, Chief Comatzi of the Kalapalos gave a very detailed account to his own people, describing their predecessors' encounter with Fawcett, and in which he reminded the tribe exactly how their forefathers had killed the three white men.

However, while the persistent rumours that Fawcett was butchered by unfriendly natives makes for a thrilling and cinematic piece of storytelling, perhaps the real explanation is a far simpler one. German anthropologist Max Schmidt, who visited Mato Grosso in 1928 and 1929, always put forward a more prosaic explanation. His extensive knowledge of the region and of the many natives he encountered, including the

Paresí, Bacairí, Kaiabi, Paresí, Iranches and Umotinas tribes convinced him that the three men had simply entered the impenetrable forests, become lost and disorientated, and starved to death. By refusing to give any details of his intended route, Fawcett simply made it impossible for anyone to find him.

Indeed, the Brazilian Indian Service deeply regretted that Fawcett, who was obsessively secretive, had not requested their assistance in dealing with the Indians. There are still over 400 indigenous tribes in the Amazon, each with their own culture and language. So determined was Fawcett to play his cards close to his chest, that perhaps he grossly underestimated the help he needed.

Unlike a Hollywood whodunit, the story of Percy Fawcett has no convenient happy ending. It is, however, every bit as cryptic and mysterious. In that case, perhaps the final word in the enigmatic and rather numinous story of the real Indiana Jones, and his search for the legendary lost city, should belong not to an archaeologist, but to one of the many occultists and spiritualists, who firmly believed that Fawcett never intended to return from the Amazon at all, but instead planned to set up a commune and communicate with another dimension through a secret gateway or portal he had discovered inside a cave deep in the Roncador Mountains.

The 1996 expedition, led by James Lynch, a Brazilian financier, hoped to finally uncover the location of 'Z' and the final resting place of Percy Fawcett, in a journey which his party dubbed *'The greatest exploration mystery of the twentieth century.'* Like many others who have tried, both before and since, they were warned by a mystic they encountered living near the Roncador mountain range,

'You will never find the lost city or the white explorer, as long as you look for them in this world.'

Although Percy Fawcett undoubtedly lost his life while searching for his very own Temple of Doom somewhere in the vast and impenetrable Brazilian jungle, we may never know precisely when, how, or where he finally disappeared. His determination to never reveal his secret treasure map ensured that he would never be found. Fawcett's earthly remains seem destined to be lost forever, like the mysterious city he sought and died for.

'We do not follow maps to buried treasure, and X never, ever, marks the spot.'
Indiana Jones, *in 'Indiana Jones and the Last Crusade'*

Scan here for extra photographs and digital versions of the images contained in this chapter

El Dorado – The Search for the Lost City

In Search of the Real Indiana Jones

Indiana Jones and the Dial of Destiny

More About Amazon Tribes from Survival International

The Famous Opening
Sequence to Raiders
of the Lost Ark

The Story Behind the
Lost City of Z

The Search Continues:

For more information, simply scan the QR codes below:

World Overview of Missing Persons Data

MissingPeople.org (UK Charity Statistics)

National Crime Agency Missing Persons Unit

(It is possible to search UK cases and updates here)

US Government National Missing
Persons Database

F.B.I. Missing Persons Database

DOE Network – An International
Missing Persons Database

Never Quit Looking (A Global
Database of cases)

Exclusive Bonus Story

Scan here to read *A Day at the Beach,* the story of an Australian tragedy:

Exclusive Competition

Please scan the QR code below and enter your details to take part in an exclusive competition only available through this book.

Your name will be then entered into a draw to receive a hamper of goodies, books and tokens, all ERASED and book related, and including a rare first edition!

Only one entry per person. Competition expires on 31 December 2023. The winner will be notified by email shortly afterwards.

Brindle Books Ltd

We hope that you have enjoyed this book. To find out more about Brindle Books Ltd, including news of new releases, please visit our website:

http://www.brindlebooks.co.uk

There is a contact page on the website, should you have any queries, and you can let us know if you would like email updates of news and new releases. We promise that we won't spam you with lots of sales emails, and we will never sell or give your contact details to any third party.

If you purchased this book online, please consider leaving an honest review on the site from which you purchased it. Your feedback is important to us, and may influence future releases from our company.

To view our current releases, please scan the QR code below:

Printed in Great Britain
by Amazon